Crosscurrents / MODERN CRITIQUES

Harry T. Moore, *General Editor*

PADRAIC COLUM
A Biographical-Critical Introduction

Zack Bowen

WITH A PREFACE BY
Harry T. Moore

SOUTHERN ILLINOIS UNIVERSITY PRESS
Carbondale and Edwardsville

FEFFER & SIMONS, INC.
London and Amsterdam

Contents

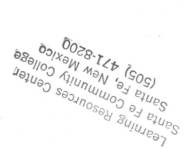

In presenting this first comprehensive treatment of
Padraic Colum and his work, Zack Bowen has supplied
something that has long been needed, and in doing so
has given us what is in its own right a good book.

Padraic Colum—I remember first reading him in high
school, in the 1920's. In those days, high-school boys
could virtually acquire a university education in the
humanities by reading those tiny, 64-page paperbacks,
"the Little Blue Books," published by E. Haldeman-
Julius in Girard, Kansas, for ten cents a copy. In one of
them I read an essay about Padraic Colum. The book was
by Llewelyn Powys; I can't recall whether it was in
Honey and Gall or Cup-Bearers of Wine and Hellebore,
but it was persuasive enough to induce me to spend my
allowance on a copy of the slim green volume of Wild
Earth which the Macmillan Company fortunately kept
in print. I was sharply aware of my family's Irish background and was just discovering for myself the Irish
Renaissance. I can never forget the effect upon my consciousness of such poems as "The Plower," "The Old
Woman of the Roads," or "A Drover," particularly three
stanzas of that last poem:

> To Meath of the pastures,
> From wet hills by the sea,
> Through Leitrim and Longford,
> Go my cattle and me.

. . . .

Then the wet, winding roads,
Brown bogs with black water;
And my thoughts on white ships
And the King o'Spain's daughter.

. . . .

And the crowds at the fair,
The herds loosened and blind,
Loud words and dark faces
And the wild blood behind.

To appreciate such poetry you don't have to be an adolescent trying to realize his Irish heritage.

Many years after Wild Earth had first moved me, I read Colum's novel, The Flying Swans, with enjoyment and admiration. As Zack Bowen points out in the present book, Colum took ten years to write this novel, his second. "The only major critic" who spoke out for it was Van Wyck Brooks, who called it "a moving and beautiful evocation of an Irish boyhood in a timeless world of country sights and sounds." Professor Bowen tells us that Colum had planned the volume as the first part of a trilogy, but that the lack of response to it discouraged him. This is another sad commentary on the present state of literary affairs, particularly when book-review editors and their contributors don't sufficiently recognize good writing and give so much space to discussions of the bad. (I remember reviewing the book favorably, though I can't recall where; it was probably for Alice Dixon Bond, the literary editor of the Boston Herald.)

I never expected to have the pleasure of meeting Padraic Colum, but I did on several occasions, and once when I was going to Dublin he kindly gave me introductions to some of his friends there. I had seen and met him first at the Bloomsday 1961 meeting of the James Joyce Society at the Gotham Book Mart, whose enthusiastic proprietor, Frances Steloff, has done so much for the cause of modern literature. On that occasion, Padraic Colum started the evening's program with some lively reminiscences of the man he called "Jice," who had included several friendly lines about "young Colum" in Ulysses, mentioning the poem "A Drover."

At the end of that Gotham evening, Dr. Steloff passed out glasses of a yellow Swiss wine that was Joyce's favorite. (I've noted elsewhere that, although the readers of D. H. Lawrence are supposed to be cultists, they have no such rituals as this!) The main part of that Bloomsday program featured a young man from the faculty of one of the New York State universities. A trained musician, he had found the musical hints and references in Ulysses of compelling interest and had supervised a fascinating dramatization of the Lestrygonians episode, with music suggested by the text itself.

That evening he played us a recording of his dramatization. This and other episodes from Ulysses which he has treated in similar fashion are now published by Folkways Records. The young man I am speaking of is of course Zack Bowen.

A few years after that pleasant Bloomsday experience, he suggested the present volume, which we are happy to have in the Crosscurrents series. It is an attractively personal book, giving us a full picture of Padraic Colum as well as of his various writings. And they are various; as Professor Bowen points out, Padraic Colum has more than one public, and the members of some units don't know of the work appreciated by those of others. Zack Bowen's book deals with all these phases, giving us new perspectives. And he is not one of those commentators who merely interpret; he is usefully critical throughout. This deepens the value of his study of an Irish writer who has lived in America since 1914 but who revisits his native land almost every year. He has appropriately been honored in both these countries by their institutes of arts and letters (including the medal of the American Irish historical society for "eminence in literature"), and now he is the subject of Zack Bowen's valuable book. Among other things, it helps to make apparent the continuing and essentially Irish vision of Padraic Colum, which has the sense of magic livingness that Yeats defined in his important essay, "The Celtic Element in Literature." This Celtic quality has greatly helped Colum in his renditions of folk tales and epics for children, but *it has also served to give life to his writing in general, his poems and plays and fiction.*

HARRY T. MOORE

Southern Illinois University
September 1, 1969

Introduction

Any author who attempts, in a single volume, to place in perspective the life and works of so active and prolific a writer as Padraic Colum must face the choice of either dealing extensively with a few of the author's works, or including greatly attenuated analyses of all the major ones. I have chosen the latter alternative, first because of the vastly different nature of the several areas of Colum's literary work and secondly because of the enormous variety of the work within each area.

Furthermore, in contrast to previous studies which consider only special aspects of Colum's career, for example, the poetry or the drama, this book aspires to treat that career comprehensively. I have discovered in conversation with people interested in poetry, for instance, that they were unaware of Colum's children's stories; I have spoken to children's librarians who never knew he wrote a play; and I have met a multitude of avid readers who could not conceive of his having written novels, biographies or essays. The primary aim of this study, then, is to present the full scope of Colum's work as well as some idea of its worth.

I sincerely appreciate Mr. Colum's help in preparing my manuscript, as well as the access he has granted me to his correspondence, his manuscripts, his books and his mind. I am greatly indebted to him for the pleasure of his company and for his patience in submitting to the detestable tape recorder. It is impossible not to appreciate his genuine humility, his unflagging humor, and his great humanity.

I wish to thank my colleagues Glenn Burne and Sheldon Grebstein for reading my manuscript and offering valuable suggestions. I am grateful to the Research Foundation of State University of New York for the grant with which I initiated the research on this project and the American Philosophical Society for the funds which enabled me to complete it. I appreciate also the cooperation of the staff of the Children's Division of the Philadelphia Public Library, and Mr. Josiah T. Newcomb, the Director of Libraries at the State University of New York at Binghamton, who facilitated the purchase of the Colum papers and manuscripts for the University. Finally I would like to acknowledge the help of my wife, without whose love, persistence, and counsel this book would never have been conceived or written.

ZACK BOWEN

Binghamton
Barnegat Light
May, 1969

Padraic Colum

1

The Collumbs of Collumbkille

The present spelling of Padraic Colum's name is an ab-
breviated Gaelic version of Patrick Collumb, the name
of Padraic's father. The origins of the Collumb family
are obscured by antiquity but the probability is that their
home, Collumbkille, was named after the family rather
than the family after the place. Donald Collumb, Padraic's paternal grandfather, was a farmer, descended from
a long line of farmers. His maternal grandfather, Richard
MacCormack, also had roots in the soil, though a far
more domesticated soil, for Mr. MacCormack was a
gardener who at one time worked in the great gardens of
Power Court. The MacCormacks lived in County Cavan as did the Connollys, Mrs. MacCormack's family.
The Connollys were to come to know little Padraic
Colum and his brothers and sisters, since it was in Cavan that the children were to stay while their father
made an abortive journey to seek fame and fortune in
America.

The MacCormacks' daughter, Susan, wed Patrick Collumb, a graduate of the national school and later a
teacher there. After the national school, Patrick took up
teaching in the workhouse in Longford and later became
the master. A workhouse is a government institution for
poor people who have been displaced from their homes.
Young Padraic was to talk, but more often listen, to the
indigents who were to pass through the workhouse all
through his early years. Colum's play *Thomas Muskerry*

and many of the characters in his poetry are all products of his workhouse days. Poverty, loss and tragedy were the common lot of these people and the majority of the characters the writer was later to create. Colum was born in the workhouse as were four of his brothers and sisters. Eight children were eventually born to Patrick and Susan. Padraic, the eldest, was born December 8, 1881, the day of the Feast of the Immaculate Conception, a sign, said Susan, that the Virgin would always smile on the youngster. His birth was followed by those of Frederick, Eileen, Donald, Maisy (who died in infancy), Richard, a second Maisy, and Susan. Three of the family still survive: Susan, who still lives in Dublin; Donald, a plasterer; and Padraic.

Young Colum's days at the workhouse were enlivened by a variegated cast of characters, the most noteworthy of them a doctor, who was a frequent visitor and a man of letters. During his visits he would hold forth on Shakespeare to the spellbound Collumbs. He was spoken of reverently by the family, for he was not only a man of great literary depth, but also a seasoned traveler, who had gone on "The Pilgrimage" to Lourdes. His affinity for literature and travel made a great impression on Padraic and kindled in the child a determination to read and to see the rest of the world.

Patrick's job, though considered eminently respectable, was not one for which the remuneration was exceptionally large. Though the family was quartered comfortably enough in the workhouse there was not a great deal of extra cash and Patrick was a man with a considerable thirst. He fell into debt and was forced finally to resign. While the children went to live with their grandmother, Ann Connolly, in County Cavan, Patrick came to the United States and journeyed west to Colorado, where he heard the streets were being paved with silver. When he found only mud there, Patrick was able to return to New York by forging a letter of recommendation from a Senator Collumb to secure himself a job transporting cattle from Colorado to New York.

While Patrick was adventuring in America, his oldest son was coming under the influence of his uncle, Micky Burns, the husband of Mrs. Collumb's sister, Mary. Mr. Burns was a buyer of fowl who traveled the countryside purchasing birds and selling them for export. It was an exciting life for Colum to accompany his uncle on his buying expeditions, meeting the country folk and haggling with the merchants at the fair. Burns was not only a man of affairs in the Cavan district, but a remarkable ballad singer who would regale his young companion with ballads and legends as they strode along the Cavan roads. A substantial part of the Colum canon of songs and stories emanated from Micky Burns. Colum was with the Connollys in Cavan for three short but exceptionally impressionable years from ages six through nine.

Meanwhile the United States in the late 1880's had fallen into an extensive economic depression, and upon Patrick's return to New York from Colorado he could find little work better than shoveling snow. Somehow he managed to save enough money to return to Ireland where he secured employment working as a clerk in the Sandy Cove Railway Station just outside Dublin. Later, when he became station master, his two eldest boys, Padraic and Fred, were hired to deliver packages for the railway.

Colum began attending school at the Glasthule national school in Sandy Cove. His school master, Denis Condon, awakened the boy's awareness and sensitivity to poetry, and in response young Colum was soon able to delight his master by reciting from memory great numbers of poems. It was a time of intense stimulation for Colum. He haunted the second-hand bookshops of Dunleary where books could be purchased for as little as a twopence or a penny. The literature he bought was not necessarily the normally prescribed academic fare, but such as would satisfy the far more varied and diverse tastes of a youngster. He attended the national school for about eight years until he was seventeen. Meanwhile he worked with his brother Fred delivering parcels after school, even for a while working full time every other day and attending school on alternate days. According to Colum the delivery job helped to shape his eventual outlook on life.

> I was fortunate in being able to help my brother deliver parcels because it took me away from what might have been that introspective [preoccupation]. I think that I had a tendency towards melancholy. If I hadn't been taken away from that and put on the streets and the roads and went around meeting people and other boys and gangs I would have been—God knows what—I don't.[1]

He was a favorite of the other boys who used to accompany him on his rounds, and he became something of a minor young celebrity in the community as he walked along behind the parcel cart reciting poems, ballads, and songs.

As the elder Collumb advanced with the railway company the lot of the family improved, but since there was a considerable proliferation of jobs in the station—clerks, ticket takers, assistants—nobody, not even the station master, was paid what could be considered a handsome salary.

When Colum was seventeen he passed his examinations and obtained a position as a clerk in the Irish Railway Clearing House on Kildare Street, Dublin. He was there for five years, working nine hours a day and writing his poems and plays in his free time. The death of his mother in 1897 signaled the dispersal of the family. The younger children went to live with Patrick's relatives in the country and in America. Padraic had always maintained contact with his relatives in County Cavan, but now, with his sisters and brothers living in the country, he spent a great deal of time in rural Ireland and his awareness of the rustic peasant tradition was kept alive through constant proximity. These visits later were to result in such poems as "The Plougher" and "The Drover."

Patrick had by this time lost his job in the railway

station and Padraic, as the eldest child, assumed responsibility for his brothers and sisters. When the children went to live in the country, some of this responsibility was alleviated and Padraic was able to devote himself increasingly to his writing.

The years of Colum's young manhood were a period of intense activity in pro-Irish cultural affairs, as the arts became a part of the great nationalistic movement which swept Ireland at the end of the nineteenth century. Colum became a duly constituted member of the Gaelic League, an organization promoting the revival of the Irish culture and language. The militant Irish Republican Army was secretly training and the young poet dutifully drilled with his close friend Arthur Griffith.

With the inception of the Irish Literary Renaissance the atmosphere around Dublin became charged with excitement and enthusiasm. It was a wonderful time to be young and a poet. There were no barriers to acknowledgment and fame for an aspiring artist. The great figures of the age were on the scene and accessible. Mary Colum tells us, "Between Abbey Street and College Green, a five minutes' walk, one could meet every person of importance in the life of the city at a certain time in the afternoon." [2]

Everywhere people were trying to reëstablish contact with their roots and traditions. For this Colum found himself almost uniquely qualified. Unlike Yeats, AE, Lady Gregory and Synge, Colum knew the Irish peasants they were talking and writing about. For one thing his Irish Roman Catholic background gave him insights into the minds of the predominantly Catholic Irish peasantry which Yeats and the other Protestants could acquire only indirectly through study and inference. His early days at the workhouse and with Michael Burns and the Connollys in the country provided in Colum's poetry and plays a basis for authenticity which the other writers of the movement were trying, sometimes vainly, to imitate. Colum was and still is a poet of the people, and it was exactly this kind of poet which was demanded by those days of the Irish cultural revival. Consequently, it was not long before his poems got into print. His first works were published in *The Irish Independent* and in Arthur Griffith's *United Irishman*. His best early poems, notably "The Plougher," "The Drover," and "The Poor Scholar," appeared first in Griffith's paper. It was the last of these that excited much praise and attracted the attention of Yeats. Colum had become overnight a well-known poet.

Through Griffith, Colum joined an Irish literary society called *Cumann na nGaedeal*. The society offered a prize of three guineas for a play which would propagandize against Irishmen enlisting in the British army. Colum's play *The Saxon Shillin'* won the competition. The title of the play was a commonly used contemptuous term for the payment made to those who had sold out to the British. Colum had, of course, a personal stake in the play, since his nearest brother, Fred, had indeed taken the Saxon shilling himself. The play was published in the *United Irishman* and subsequently produced. Through the production of the play Colum met the Fay brothers, who were attempting to bring Irish Nationalism to the theatre. So began a love affair with the theatre which has remained undiminished to this day.

Colum was invited by the Fays to join the group, which went by the title The National Theatre Society. It was a cooperative, democratic organization in which the members themselves worked in all facets of production from writing to acting. Colum was often called upon to pick up a spear and join the cast. The democracy in the group, which permitted everyone a say in choosing which plays were to be staged, finally resulted in its undoing, for the veto of one of its most puritanical members might and finally did result in the society's refusal to produce the work of a genius such as Synge.

It was through this group that Colum got to know Yeats, whose own Irish Literary Theatre had failed and who was interested in having the new Fay company produce his plays. Yeats attended rehearsals from time to time and thus struck up an acquaintance with Colum which was, through the unintentional aid of an uncharitable critic, to solidify into lifelong friendship. Following is Colum's account of the affair:

> I had written a piece in the *United Irishman* which some correspondent denounced—saying "What sort of stuff is this nonsense that these young people are writing?" One day in the Irish Railway Clearing House I was told somebody had come to see me, and I went out and there was Yeats at the door—Yeats! This strange man who must have looked very strange walking down Kildare Street. He had come to tell me that he was going to back me up in this piece . . . writing letters and so on. He was wonderful, and very much impressed by [my poem] "The Poor Scholar."

Yeats took the younger man under his wing and introduced him to Lady Gregory, who held court at the Nassau Hotel when she was in Dublin.

During this period Colum produced a successful play, *Broken Soil* (1903), and became a frequenter of the Hermetic Society. The group, followers of Madame Blavatsky, made sojourns into the occult world. Colum's interest in the group, however, was more for the association with such personages as Maud Gonne and AE than for its theosophy. He was accepted also into AE's Sunday night gatherings, heady company for a writer still in his early twenties. He began a rigorous schedule of reading in the National Library. Living by himself on the South Circular Road, with few distractions, he wrote some of his best poetry in his next few years. Such memorable poems as "The Plougher," "The Ballad Singer," and "Dermott Donne MacMorna," written during this period of close contact with the Irish theatre are character pieces which bear the heavy imprint of the dramatist.

Colum's financial fortunes took a turn for the better when he met Thomas Hughes Kelly at Lady Gregory's. Kelly, the son of a wealthy American banker, Eugene

Kelly, had decided to establish a number of scholarships for promising Irish writers and scholars. He was told that young Colum would be a deserving choice, and Kelly contracted to pay for a five-year period of study, development and writing for Colum. Padraic was to receive his current yearly salary from the Clearing House, £70 the first year, with the stipend to increase £10 a year for the following four years. It was the realization of a dream for the aspiring writer. He was now able to devote full time to his literary work and produced a harvest of articles, plays, and poems during this period.

Meanwhile all was not quiet on the theatrical front. The National Theatre Society consisted of strong-willed, highly individualistic people and there were more than enough arguments to keep the pot boiling. Colum was to come in for his share early. When the *Saxon Shillin'* was offered, Fay did not want to put it on without a few changes to make it seem less political. Colum consented to revise the ending, thus incurring the wrath of the fiercely nationalistic Maud Gonne, Griffith and others. Maud Gonne subsequently wrote Colum a letter castigating him for his "enslaved mind," and it was some time before the two were on speaking terms again.

Colum's play *Broken Soil* achieved success in Dublin and went on to London as a part of the Theatre Society repertoire, along with plays by Yeats and Synge. Yeats and Lady Gregory disapproved of including the play in the London tour on the grounds that the work was immature, an opinion with which Colum now whole-heartedly concurs. But the Theatre Society democracy prevailed; after all, Colum was one of the group and the play would be put on. Ironically its London performance won far more critical applause than Yeats's play, mainly, according to Colum, because people misunderstood it. Later the play was rewritten and became *The Fiddler's House*.

Rifts like these were so numerous that when Miss Elizabeth Horniman offered to buy a place for a new theatre on Abbey Street, Yeats and company were more than ready to agree. The new group moved into a little place formerly called the Mechanics Theatre, in a building part of which previously had been the morgue—according to Colum a "very inauspicious beginning." The first plays produced in the winter and spring of 1904–05 were those of Yeats, Synge, Lady Gregory and William Boyle, but Colum's *The Land*, produced June 9, 1905, achieved the first popular acclaim, mainly because his play was eminently understandable and dealt with an important historical occasion.

It was inevitable that such a volatile group would not stay together long. There was the nationalistic segment, who felt that Irish plays had no business on the London stage; and there was Miss Horniman herself, a relatively tactless lady who demanded as a condition to her gift of the theatre that the democratic traditions established by Frank Fay be abolished. There was to be no voting on which plays were to be produced, but instead the decisions were to come from a reading group of three, Yeats, Synge, and Fay. This group alone was empowered to pass on the plays. A few people left immediately and more followed, including Padraic Colum. Colum's resignation stemmed less from the new voting procedure than from an intemperate letter from the pen of Miss Horniman, who asserted that "Colum will stay because he knows which side his bread is buttered on." This, of course, prompted his resignation.

He joined a short-lived secessionist group called the Theatre of Ireland. *The Fiddler's House*, a rewriting of the earlier *Broken Soil*, originally intended for the Abbey Theatre, was given to the new Theatre of Ireland group and produced in 1907. However, the last play that Colum wrote for the National Theatre movement, *Thomas Muskerry*, was put on by the Abbey in 1910.

During this period he met and courted Mary Catherine Gunning Maguire (later affectionately called Molly), a lovely, saucy, bright student at University College, Dublin. After graduation she taught at St.

Enda's, one of two schools operated by Padraic Pearse, for whose institutions Colum also delivered occasional lectures. Molly joined her future husband, James Stephens and two other members of Pearse's staff, Thomas MacDonagh and David Houston, in forming *The Irish Review*. Colum in a recent issue of *The Dublin Magazine* describes the inception of the periodical:

> David Houston was an outgoing, enthusiastic, hospitable man, with a tinge of Orangism that was provocative. Now his house open on Sunday afternoons was crammed with Irish Revivalists. Thomas MacDonagh from the school down the road appeared amongst them. So did James Stephens, who was now a cherished guest at every reception in Dublin. I would come with M. C. M. [Molly], who was a favourite in the Houston household.
>
> One evening the sanguine householder announced to the four of us that he had the establishment of an Irish monthly in mind. It is a measure of the faith that obtained in those days that this disclosure was discussed, not merely seriously, but eagerly. Houston, MacDonagh, Stephens and myself were to conduct it. We named the future publication—at my suggestion, I think—*The Irish Review*. M. C. M. was to have the office of critic-in-chief. And the Review, mind you, was not to be quarterly, but monthly, with the same number of pages as a quarterly of today, and to be sold for sixpence.
>
> In a couple of weeks we had assembled the first number of *The Irish Review*. James Stephens' contribution to its contents was outstanding: It was the story he had just finished, his first important one, *The Charwoman's Daughter*, which he bestowed on the publication as a serial. George Moore, A. E. and Padraic Pearse gave us material.[3]

The *Review*, which was to have a distinguished voice in Irish letters, ran until November, 1914. Both MacDonagh and Pearse had only a few brief years left before they were executed following the Easter Rebellion in 1916.

The personalities of the future Mr. and Mrs. Colum were complementary in many ways. While they had, of course, their common interest in literature, Colum's attitude tended toward humility and Molly's toward arrogance. Molly's mind was essentially critical rather than creative. Even though she espoused the creed of the emancipated woman, she was exceptionally impressed by the great figures of the political and artistic world, and thrived on the company of celebrities. Her biography, *Life and the Dream*, is really as much a history of her association with great personages as it is a recounting of her life.

She was an exciting person to be near, exuding vibrancy and commitment to intellectual and artistic causes. Colum was very much in love with her. Her charming account of his proposal reveals as much about herself as about their relationship.

I did not have any taste for exchanging the independent and interesting life I was living for pottering around a kitchen, planning meals, hanging curtains, and so on, and I let my young men friends know my sentiments about this. One of them, however, declined to listen to me and kept assuring me that he was the person Heaven had destined me to marry and that I could not escape my fate. I always thought, as he was a very fine and courageous person, that he would be a nice man for somebody else to marry, which was what eventually happened—in fact he married before I did. But he made one final determined effort before dropping me. He called at my little flat, armed with an engagement ring, and told me in a very cave-man manner that he had arranged everything, that I was to marry him on a certain date in a certain church, and that I had better accept my destiny. The argument that ensued reduced me to a state of panic such as I had never known, for I was afraid I might be unable to hold out, especially as he said I had encouraged him and ought to have some sense of responsibility about it. But I managed to be strong-minded, and the harassing interview ended with tears on both sides, with his throwing the ring into the fire and leaving in a high state of emotion. I was stretched out in a condition of copious weeping when, some minutes later, another of my young men friends, a well-known Abbey author, Padraic Colum, called. Tearfully I told him of my ordeal; the ring was still lying unconsumed in a corner of the grate; he fished it out with a tongs, left it on the hearthstone to cool so that it could be mailed back to the young man who had brought it; then he settled himself gravely in an armchair and proceeded to lecture me. "I think," said he, "that to save yourself trouble, you should marry me. Then these fellows will all leave you alone and you won't have to go through any more of these scenes." He pursued this train of reasoning, and eventually I dried my eyes and said, "All right, Colum; maybe that would be best."

At the end of this scene I think he was a very sober young man at finding himself engaged to be married, for I imagine he had pondered on the marriage state about as little as I had.[4]

Contrary to the impression of a rather casual and passionless relationship conveyed by Molly's account of the proposal, their letters reflect their deep feeling and the two were practically inseparable for nearly three years before they finally married in 1912.

After a honeymoon in England, the Colums settled in a cottage in Donnybrook, where they began the habit of holding open house once a week for their literary friends, a habit continued for the rest of their lives, and one which established intimate contacts with most of the important writers in twentieth-century America and Europe. Their guests during this period included just about everyone connected with the Irish Renaissance. Their particularly close associations at the time were with AE, Sarah Purser, and James Stephens.

In addition to his literary interests, Colum was still an active militant. He joined the Irish Volunteers and took part in a celebrated gunrunning escapade in 1913; but his active participation in the Irish war effort was to be short-lived. The agreement for the yearly stipend from Kelly now expired and the couple faced exceptionally hard times on what little Colum was able to pick up free-lance writing. Josephine Colum, an aunt, offered to pay their fare to the United States, and in 1914 the couple, practically penniless, embarked for America.

When the Colums came to the United States they

went immediately to stay with Aunt Josephine in Pittsburgh. Through Harold Geoghegan, the nephew of their friend Sarah Purser, Colum got a commission from Carnegie Institute to help in the production of some Irish plays, so that almost from the start fortunes in America were better than those they had left behind in Ireland. They stayed for three months in Pittsburgh before moving to New York. There was a little tiff with the British officials who did not necessarily relish Colum's propagandizing for the Irish independence movement. He delivered several militant lectures and published some pieces in the *Gaelic American*, a paper active in the Fenian movement, but his patriotic activities on behalf of Irish nationalism were to a large extent hampered by the British, who caused the cancellations of several lectures.

The Colums lived on not-yet-stylish Beekman Place in New York and easily developed an entire new circle of literary acquaintances. Colum began to attend the meetings of the Poetry Society of America and met Robert Frost, who was to be the first of his many friends among American writers. Frost and Colum were to maintain a close, steady relationship over the years. When the lease on the Beekman Place apartment expired in 1915, the Colums journeyed to the Midwest where Colum had some lecture engagements. They stayed in Chicago with Harriet Moody, the widow of poet William Vaughn Moody. The company at the Moody home to welcome the Colums included some of the important people in the midwestern literary movement, notably Carl Sandburg, Sherwood Anderson, Vachel Lindsay, and Edgar Lee Masters.

Other literary associations were formed at the MacDowell Colony to which they came through the influence of Edwin Arlington Robinson, then a permanent summer fixture there. The Colony, in Peterboro, New Hampshire, was founded in honor of Edward MacDowell by his wife, and is a summer camp for artists, musicians and writers. Among the literary figures present were Hervey Allen, Du Bose Heyward, and Elinor Wylie, who was later to become a neighbor in New Canaan. The Colums spent the summers of 1917 and 1918 there, returning again in 1923 after they came back from Hawaii. Much of Colum's first novel, *Castle Conquer*, was written at MacDowell, as well as a number of his Hawaiian stories.

Both Colum and his wife were publishing occasional pieces, while Molly also had a job as a private tutor briefly before going to work as a translator and editorial and fashion writer for *Women's Wear*, a daily fashion journal. About this time a major turn of events was about to take place in Colum's career. It was to have an inauspicious beginning with Miss Betsy Brewer's offer of eight dollars a week for some stories to be printed in the children's column of the New York *Sunday Tribune*. The series became the basis of Colum's first extensive volume of children's stories, *The King of Ireland's Son* (1916). The appearance of this first volume was made possible by Willy Pogany, a Hungarian artist and illustrator. Pogany mentioned to Colum that he would very much like to illustrate a book of Irish stories and, as Colum had been working on the stories for the *Tribune*, the two agreed to collaborate on *The King of Ireland's Son*. Pogany's publisher, Holt, also readily agreed to issue an American edition of *Wild Earth* (1916), a collection of Colum's poetry previously published in 1907. The two volumes firmly established Colum in the United States.

The Macmillan Company at that time was a family establishment managed by a perceptive Englishman, George Brett. Having read *The King of Ireland's Son*, Brett offered Colum a contract with Macmillan's, initiating a relationship which despite its ups and downs is still flourishing. Brett's idea was to employ Colum on a regular stipend basis in exchange for two volumes a year, one a fairly extensive treatment for children of one of the great sagas, myths, or classics of the Western Civilization, and the other a shorter book of stories for younger children. For several years the arrangement worked admirably, mainly through the efforts of the children's editor, Miss Louise Seaman. Over the years nineteen books have followed *The King of Ireland's Son* (which Macmillan subsequently took over from Holt) in that highly successful series, and the Colums were freed for a while at least from economic pressures.

The Colums' triumphant return to Ireland in 1922 was marred by the news, which reached them on the boat, of the death of Colum's old friend Arthur Griffith. For Padraic, who had expected to find Griffith at the head of the new Free State, the shock was deep, and was compounded by still another shock at the death of Michael Collins. Though they were received most cordially by the new President of the Free State, William Cosgrave, and the head of the army, General Richard Mulcahy, many of the people who had known and worked with Colum in his formative years were gone, and for him the country was never to be quite the same. Some years after, at the insistence of Desmond Fitzgerald and Griffith's political party, Colum took on the task of a biography of Griffith, but the work was set aside and pursued only at intervals, until it was finally finished in 1959. Though he was in Ireland only a few months in 1922, Colum found time to edit a collection of Welsh stories, *The Island of the Mighty*, for Macmillan and to produce a play, *Grasshopper*, on which he had earlier collaborated.

The Colums continued on to Paris where Thomas Kelly, Colum's former benefactor, was staying. They remained for several months before returning to the United States en route to a new adventure in Hawaii. Just before he left for Europe, Colum had been contacted by the Hawaiian legislature. Hawaii was being infiltrated with more and more immigrants of all nationalities and the government wanted someone to collect a volume of authentic Polynesian poems, stories, and legends, which would provide a background of national folk tradition for children in the Hawaiian schools. The legislature contacted a number of publishers and were finally referred to Colum. Colum's own version of the Hawaiian venture really cannot be improved upon.

Through the children's stories I became an authority on folklore without ever telling anybody I was one. . . .

We were in Paris. And we took a boat from Paris to New York. We took a train from New York to San Francisco. We took a liner from San Francisco to Honolulu and when we got there they put a lei on our necks. They got us a little cottage down on Waikiki, and we settled down without thinking of anything beyond that. And then one evening I went into Honolulu; I remember great winds blowing, coconuts knocking me on the head along the street, and I suddenly realized: "What the hell am I doing here? What do I expect to do? Where is it? I don't know a word of the language; I don't know the history of the people; and here I am, going to write about them!" It was then I told Molly we'd better slip off to Australia, that I had a brother there who'd cover up for me. "No," she said. She was always of the opinion that I had this self-confidence that should be pricked at some time or another. "Now's the time to get your self-confidence. That should show you what t'will lead you to. No, you are not going to Australia. You'll have to stay here." So I did and worked it out.

It was curious and interesting too how I got started on it. I was groping around and I went into the Bishop Museum; that's the museum of Polynesian stuff in Honolulu. I didn't notice anything very interesting as I was going along. Then I saw the feathered capes. You know the high chieftains wore what you'd call now a stole just around their shoulders, and it was made of feathers, feathers stitched on tapa and it went over the shoulders. They were generally in black, yellow, red, and they were only permitted to take one feather out of a bird and let it go, so it must have taken twenty years to make a cape of that kind. It was that that gave me the impression that I wanted of this strange civilization that was trying to matter, and then I began to learn some of the language. The very fact that there was a civilization in which a man would spend twenty years trying to make a cape . . . that's what impressed me. So that's how it happened. In three months I was lecturing the Hawaiian Academy on their traditions. Now isn't that something? My self-confidence still lasted. After that terrible discovery of mine that I knew nothing, to have enough self-confidence left to lecture to the Hawaiian Academy on the traditions— why my god! When I think about it! Molly used to say that I'd undertake to do anything except earn a living.

Of course, Colum's account does not do justice to the fact that his knowledge of Hawaiian lore was established only after painstaking research. He worked for months in the Bishop Museum with Hawaiian scholars and then scoured the remote sections of Hawaii for songs and legends, calling at nearly all of the islands including the leper island, Molokai. His Hawaiian endeavors resulted in two volumes: *At the Gateways of the Day* (1924), and *The Bright Islands* (1925), published by Yale University Press. The books were later combined into one volume, *Legends of Hawaii* (1937). Meanwhile Macmillan had published a novel, *Castle Conquer* (1923) and a volume of poetry, *Dramatic Legends and Other Poems* (1922).

Colum's stature as a folklorist as well as a dramatist and poet now firmly established, the Colums returned via Europe to New York for a time and then in 1925 moved into their first permanent home, which Elinor Wylie found for them in New Canaan, Connecticut. Molly was now well known as a critic and wrote extensively for the New York *Times* and *Tribune*. During this period Colum produced a remarkable string of books, including *The Voyagers* (1925), *The Forge in the Forest* (1925), *The Road Round Ireland* (1926), *Creatures* (poems, 1927), *The Fountain of Youth* (1927), *Balloon* (a play, 1929) and *Orpheus* (1930).

In 1929 Colum tried another fling at the theatre by attempting to have his play, *Balloon*, produced. He recalls:

> I wrote a play for Broadway, called *Balloon*. It's still called the most famous unproduced play on Broadway. It was bought by Michael Myerberg. He had just put on Thornton Wilder's *Our Town*. He was enterprising and avant-garde. He got my play and put it on over in Ogun-

quit—experimentally—and it was a success. It ran not only
for a week but for two weeks, which had never happened
before. And then after I had imagined myself as making
money on Broadway it never went on. The usual disap-
pointment. . . . So I'm a foiled, frustrated dramatist.

Though the Colums stayed for only three years in
New Canaan, these were particularly enjoyable, trouble-
free years, enriched by friends and interspersed with
weekly visits to New York City. In Connecticut they
became part of a distinguished social circle, including
such literary figures as the Eugene O'Neills (whose
daughter Oona was named by Molly), Van Wyck
Brooks, Elinor Wylie and her husband William Rose
Benét, Bliss Carman, Michael Monahan, Hendrik Van
Loon, and Maxwell Perkins, who was especially impressed with Molly and published her first book, *From
These Roots*, in 1937.

But the life of New Canaan finally proved too quiet
for the couple when dynamic things were happening in
the literary world outside, especially in Paris. Accord-
ingly, the Colums embarked for France in 1930, and
were there when the Great Depression overtook them.
The stipend from Macmillan came to an end. Despite
his earlier cordial relations with Macmillan Company,
Colum was too much an Irishman to submit gently to
this interruption of his income. Following is part of the
text of his letter to H. S. Latham of Macmillan's. The
letter is dated July 14, 1932.

> Your letter and telegram mean that the Macmillan Co.
> are leaving me, an author who has given them twenty
> books, without any income whatever. And on what pre-
> tence? That I have a deficit of 2709 dollars. . . . I shall not
> forget that the Macmillan co. are more anxious to take a
> stand on their auditors' report rather than on their au-
> thor's interest. I should like to remind them that publish-
> ers live by authors, not by auditors. If their authors get
> disgusted with them or are forced into other ways of
> earning a living, what good will their auditors be to them?
> . . . If Macmillans withhold the total earnings on my

books I shall have the matter debated in the literary journals of America and Europe. . . . I propose that you make me an allowance of one hundred dollars per month with a thousand dollars advance on my new book, "Other Roads in Ireland." If you are willing to do this cable me on receipt of this letter.

Colum's protestations were not entirely in vain. A small stipend was forthcoming, but once again the Colums found themselves in financial straits. Their difficulties were compounded when it was discovered that Molly must undergo a very serious operation. She had never been exceptionally healthy, attributing her numerous illnesses to an internal childhood injury suffered in a fall from a horse.[5] It was during this six months' stay in Paris, however, that their memorable association with James Joyce flourished. This friendship was described at length in their biography, *Our Friend James Joyce* (1958).

When it became apparent that Molly's convalescence from her operation was going to take some time, they moved to Nice. There were a few reviews to keep them going and eventually Macmillan granted advances on two books, *The Big Tree of Bunlahy* (1933) and *The White Sparrow* (1933), both of which Colum completed on the Riviera. Because Nice was a cheaper place to live than Paris, the Colums' financial picture began to brighten, prompting the following assessment from Mary:

> I think nowhere in the world could life be pleasanter, easier, and cheaper than on the Riviera at the time. Owing to the crash and the near failure of many publishing houses, our income had been reduced by something like seventy per cent, yet we lived almost as well on the reduced monthly sum his publishers paid my husband, though we had little to spare for clothes or extras. My husband never got so much work done.[6]

Fortunately Molly's recuperation progressed rapidly and in 1933 she was offered a literary editorship in *The Forum*, a position she retained until the periodical was suspended in 1940.

With the recovery of Molly's health and the offer of the *Forum* editorship, the Colums moved back to New York and into the Beekman Towers Hotel. They remained in New York for the rest of their lives, except for visits back to Europe, and a brief sojourn in Norwalk, Connecticut. Molly's regular salary as editor was augmented by Colum's publication of four more books before 1940: *The Legend of Saint Columba* (1935), *The Story of Lowry Maen* (a long narrative poem, 1937), *Flower Pieces* (poems, 1938), and *Where the Winds Never Blew and the Cocks Never Crew* (1940). After the *Forum* expired, Molly still contributed to *The Dial, Scribners, New Republic, New Statesman and Nation, Yale Review* and other periodicals.

The Colums' interim move to Norwalk was short and ill-fated. Molly was struck by a car and seriously injured, prompting their return to New York City. They lived for a time on Claremont Avenue, but Molly, unsatisfied with the place, found them a Central Park West apartment convenient to Columbia University. Colum still resides there.

It was just after World War II that the Arthur Griffith biography, which Colum had started twenty years earlier, suddenly began again to play a part in his life. Griffith's party in Ireland was anxious to see the biography published, as much for political motives as for patriotism. Joseph McGrath, "The Only Irish Tycoon," financed a trip back to Dublin for the Colums so that Colum could finish his research on the manuscript. They stayed for several months with sister Susan while the research was in progress and returned to the United States with a trunk full of notes but still no completed manuscript. It would be still another ten years before the Griffith book would appear. When we discussed the biography, Colum recalled the delay, but not the reasons for it.

> There was a great deal of hesitation about it. First of all I started it and then Macmillans gave me advances for it, and then I didn't get on with it for some reason . . . I've forgotten why. [Later] they renewed their pressure from

Dublin, and I felt in my conscience that I should do it. Soon there wouldn't be anybody left who knew Arthur Griffith and understood what he was up to. So I did it. But then I didn't publish the book until after Molly's death.

In addition to joining the faculty at Columbia in 1939, both of the Colums taught at various times at the University of Wisconsin (Madison) and at the University of Miami in Florida. In 1940 Colum received a semester appointment as visiting professor of English at City College of New York. Their longest teaching affiliation was, however, with Columbia, where until 1956 they gave a course in comparative literature.

William Spanos remembers that it was like no other graduate course he had known. Accustomed to the usual graduate school emphasis upon classics, essential minor works, and strict documentation drawn from secondary sources, he never could adapt himself to the informal literary discussions (or rather arguments) between the two instructors conducting the course. Spanos remembers Molly as a huge woman, looming over her husband, probably because she usually won the arguments. The evenings were highly personal, spiced with first-hand accounts of associations with the great writers of the late nineteenth and twentieth centuries. Colum's association with Columbia reached its culmination in 1958 when the University awarded him an honorary degree. He describes with his usual candor his role as an educator.

We were teaching in Columbia, Molly and I, in the Philosophy Department . . . and it wasn't philosophy at all. I'm not a good teacher . . . I was never meant to be a teacher because I had no training. Molly was the good teacher. She had good training in teaching. I would come in and talk to them informally rather than formally. Well, I could always teach them poetry, you know. The business of teaching poetry is to make them interested in it, isn't it? Not about the meters which I never could understand.

Having permanently established themselves in Central Park West, the Colums were subsequently offered a summer place in Woods Hole, Massachusetts by Mrs. Murray Crane, a long-standing friend of the family. Colum gave lectures, readings, and classes at Mrs. Crane's house in Woods Hole and still found plenty of time to write. The Colums, and after Molly's death Colum himself, continued to spend their summers in the picturesque Cape Cod town.

The atmosphere at Woods Hole has proved not only congenial but exceptionally productive. Colum wrote *The Flying Swans* (1957) there, as well as a number of children's books. He and Molly collaborated on the Joyce biography in Woods Hole, working independently on sections and then reviewing and criticizing each other's work. Molly had gotten the contract for the book and was particularly engrossed in it. She was still working on Joyce memoirs the morning she died. After her death Colum included her notes in the book.

Since her accident in Norwalk, Molly had been plagued with chronic arthritis and hypertension and her health began gradually to decline until her death in 1957. Her passing, though Colum had been prepared for it for some time, was the greatest shock he ever experienced, and one he still mentions only with difficulty and pain. His life has been considerably eased since Molly's death by the kindness of her nephew Emmet Greene, also an editor and writer, who came to live with Colum on the day of Molly's funeral and has looked after him ever since.

After Molly died, Colum embarked on an extensive series of lectures all over the United States for the Columbia Lecture Bureau. He has also been editing anthologies such as *Poems by Jonathan Swift* (1962), and *Poems of Samuel Ferguson* (1963).

In recent years Colum has been exceptionally busy giving lectures, presiding over the meetings of the James Joyce Society in New York, attending writers' conferences in Suffield, Connecticut, summering in Woods Hole, spending a few months each winter with his sister Susan in Ranelagh, Dublin, and in general working out of his home base in New York. His creative energies unimpaired, he has in the last decade produced, in addition to the works previously mentioned, four new books, including three volumes of poetry: *Irish Elegies* (published with additions in 1958, 1961, and 1966), *Ten Poems* (1957), and *The Poet's Circuits* (1960); and a volume of lectures, *Story Telling New and Old* (1961).

In 1961 he ventured into a quite different literary area by returning to the theatre with a series of Irish plays utilizing the Noh play form. Here he is following Yeats's precedent in adapting the form to Irish mythology. Colum, however, substitutes historical personages for Yeats's purely legendary characters. The first play in the series is *Moytura*, about Sir William Wilde. This is followed by *Glendalough*, about Parnell, *Monasterboice*, about James Joyce, and *Cloughoughter*, about Roger Casement. The later three plays, which form a trilogy, were produced by the Lantern Theatre in Dublin in 1966 under the name *The Challengers*. *Moytura* is Colum's only Noh play to have been published so far, though he has recently finished still another Noh play, *Kilmore*, about Henry Joy McCracken, an Ulster leader. The plays have satisfied a long-felt ambition. Colum says of this recent venture: "I wanted to write something short; I wanted to write something with poetry in it; and I wanted to write drama, which I'm always writing anyway."

As he approaches his eighty-seventh birthday he feels that he has a great deal more to write and too little time in which to write it. He remains alert, spritely, good-humored and eminently Irish. During a visit to our campus last year he insisted upon having a pretty co-ed sit next to him during meals. He was at his best before large audiences, reciting scores of poems from memory and recalling with ease incidents which occurred during the nineteenth century. He is still a brisk walker and a charming conversationalist.

After such a productive, distinguished career it seems almost superfluous to list the honors Padraic Colum has received; however, the following awards serve as an indication of his long service to the literary world.

1938–39	President of the Poetry Society of America
1940	Medal—Poetry Society of America
1951	Honorary Doctorate—National University of Ireland
1952	Fellowship Award—Academy of American Poets
1953	Lady Gregory Award—Academy of Irish Letters
1958	Honorary Doctorate—Columbia University
1961	Regina Medal—Catholic Library Association
1963	Membership—American Academy of Arts and Letters

2

Poetry

It is wholly proper that Padraic Colum is best known as poet, for his poems are his most significant contribution to literature. L. A. G. Strong calls him "a poet of the older tradition, one of those who regard communication as an imperative duty."[1] To dismiss Colum's style as merely straightforward, accurate, or simple, as many critics have done, is to do the craftsmanship of the poetry a considerable disservice. The way Colum says things is very often beautiful and his poetic scenes and the characters as delightful as they are unassuming and familiar. His language is unpretentious and his verse forms are predominantly lyrical and rhyming with heavily accentuated iambs and tripping anapests, the sort of poems that on first reading tend to inspire song rather than thought. As Strong's statement implies, there is no obscurantism for its own sake, no complicated syntax to unravel, few ingenious conceits to dazzle the mind, and a scarcity of literary allusions to provide grist for the scholarly mill. I suspect the forthrightness of the poet's style has been the principal cause of the dearth of literary criticism about his poetry, since the fashionable critics are now more explicative than descriptive.

Colum's subject matter and conclusions reflect the same directness. His subjects are generally common people and common sights, commemorated without bravado in their own language and terms. He describes his poetic philosophy in "The Poet":

> *But close to the ground are reared*
> *The wings that have widest sway,*
> *And the birds that sing best in the wood . . .*
> *Were reared with breasts to the clay.*[2]

Colum thinks of himself as one of the few authentic national poets of Ireland because his upbringing is rural and Catholic, as opposed to the Protestant ascendency backgrounds of poets like Yeats, AE and Lady Gregory, whose links with the peasant people are at best studied and vicarious. Much of Colum's poetry retains its roots in the Catholic peasantry of the Irish Republic, dealing occasionally with the joys and aspirations of the people but far more with their sorrows, hopelessness and disintegration. Always, however, his people are uncomplicated and readily understandable and his language sparse and accurate.

Colum cannot be considered typical of any particular modern tradition. Hailed as a poet of the Irish Renaissance, his poems lacked the nationalistic didacticism which plagued other Irish poets, whose vision of things was colored by recollections of an unblemished past and the certainty of a utopian future. During the years following World War I, a period of realism, surrealism, Dadaism and naturalism, each with its own limitations on subject matter and emphasis on a particular variety of experiment, his poems bordered on the sentimental, and were more often about the beautiful, the remote and the wondrous than the ugly, the despairing and the hopeless. The present age is returning to the inner truths of symbolism and Plato's world of forms, while Colum, unlike his contemporaries, is perfectly at home in the world as it "appears," that is, presents itself to his senses. The tendency in modern poetry is to seek the truth behind what we see, to get a meaning of the world by interpreting the objects and events around us as symbols or indicators of the truth which lies behind and above. For Colum, however, the truth of things resides in the accurate perception of them. Things are as they appear, and misunderstanding or failing to grasp their essence can only be due to faulty perception. His poetry is designed to enhance perception by clear delineation and description.

Because his poems have been generally free from the dictates of any particular literary group or theory, his work has become identified from time to time with all of them. His own declaration of freedom is embodied in his poem, "The Parrot and the Falcon."

> My Afghan poet-friend
> With this made his message end,
> "The scroll around my wall shows two the poets have
>   known—
> The parrot and falcon they—
> The parrot hangs on his spray,
> And silent the falcon sits with brooding and baleful eyes.
>
> Men come to me: one says
> 'We have given your verses praise,
> And we will keep your name abreast of the newer names;
> But you must make what accords
> With poems that are household words—
> Your own: write familiar things; to your hundred add a score.'
>
> My friend, they would bestow
> Fame for a shadow-show,
> And they would pay with praise for things dead as last year's
>   leaves.
> But I look where the parrot, stilled,
> Hangs a head with rumours filled,
> And I watch where my falcon turns her brooding and baleful
>   eyes!
>
> Come to my shoulder! Sit!
> To the bone be your talons knit!
> I have sworn my friends shall have no parrot-speech from
>   me;
> Who reads the verse I write
> Shall know the falcon's flight,
> The vision single and sure, the conquest of air and sun!
> Is there aught else worthy to weave within your banners'
>   folds?
> Is there aught else worthy to grave on the blades of your
>   naked swords?" (CP, pp. 130–31)

The chief characteristic of Colum's work, then, lies in his insistence that the ultimate truth of things does in fact lie in the world of appearances, in how they look and in what they say. Things cry out only to be observed, digested, and understood. Colum's philosophy—that the depth of understanding of the essential qualities of nature and people is accessible by merely letting down the artificial barriers to perception—is reminiscent of Thoreau's. The poet's excitement at discovering essence in appearance permeates his poem, "Ferns Castle." Inside the empty castle the poet describes his experience.

I look to where the apertures, one over one, make space
Within the massiveness of wall: such blue there never was!
Never in any place, I say, was such translucent glass!

And then the thought: how ignorant! No window pane was set
Within the depth of loop-hole that I am gazing at,
Making scrutable the figured cloth where prancing beast meets scathe.

And thereupon entrancement grew: deep, clear, unearthly
As syllables in holy words the blue was lined on high:
At Ferns Castle yesterday I looked upon the sky! [3]

Colum's continual marveling at shapes and colors is a main facet of his poetry about plants and animals. Two sizeable collections, *Creatures* (1927) and *The Vegetable Kingdom* (1954), abound in a breathless description of color and appearance. A prime example of this is "The Resplendent Quetzel-Bird," which is founded on the splendor not so much of the bird but of the color green.

Others have divers paints and enamels,
Lavish and bright on breast and wing feathers:
You, Guatemalan, have sunken all colours
Into glory of greenness!

There may be palms as greenly resplendent,
Palms by the Fountain of Youth in Anahuac—

Such greens there may be on sea-sunken bronzes—
The Gates of Callao!

There may be words in rituals spoken
To Quetzalcoatl who makes verdure through rain-flow—
Words like the gash made by knives of obsidian—
To tell of such greenness! (CP, p. 178)

The direct, honest manifestations of experience in Colum's poetry are at one time his source of excellence and the source of frustration to a literary critic attempting to deal with his work. Strong places heavy emphasis on the critic's problem.

> The work of Padraic Colum has had little critical attention, not through neglect or ignorance, but because its central quality is one with which literary criticism has little to do. Simplicity cannot be analysed. No critical instrument has been invented which will react to Colum's poetry. . . . Colum shows from time to time this child-like power to see straight to the soul of things, a power of which academic critics are frankly afraid, since it reduces poetry to its primal function of a communication from the heart of one human being to another's; and criticism, which is concerned with rationalising poetic experience, is seldom happy until such experience has been left behind. I do not wish to disparage academic criticism. It is, at its best, the metaphysics of the experience we derive from poetry. It enables us to correlate our poetic experiences, much as theology correlates religious experiences. But, like theology, it grows silent in the face of the experience itself. Thus the work of Padraic Colum, which presents us with poetic experience in its most innocent and naked form, embarrasses criticism. Often there are no allusions, no symbols, only the simplest images, nothing but the singing tone and the thing itself.[4]

Strong's comments notwithstanding, there is a significant difference between a poet's merely saying something and his saying it well. Although Colum's language and images are primarily "literal," his poetry is both meaningful and memorable. The craftsmanship which makes good poetry is not accidental, nor does it defy description. The discussion following will be an attempt to analyze and define the nature of this craftsmanship in Padraic Colum's poems.

The most marked aspect of Colum's poetry is unquestionably its lyrical quality. This becomes apparent through his use of meter and rhyme as well as his heavy utilization of the ballad stanza and refrain line.[5] Only the narrative poems, such as *The Story of Lowry Maen* and the introductions to several of the sections of *Poet's Circuits*, are not essentially strong and regular in meter. The regularity is not quite as apparent in the iambic lines as in the predominantly anapestic poems. The heavily accented three beat measure is so closely akin to ¾ time musical lines that certain poems suggest immediately their musical counterparts. For example, it is impossible for me to read "The Toy-Maker" without humming the tune of "Sweet Betsy from Pike":

> *I am the Toy-maker; I have brought from the town*
> *As much in my plack as should fetch a whole crown,*
> *I'll array for you now my stock of renown*
> *And man's the raree will show you.* (CP, p. 123)

The poet chooses to write an extraordinary number of poems in this predominantly anapestic rhythm. Although the essentially galloping nature of the rhythm would seem to place certain restrictions on the kinds of poems and subject matter which might profitably be utilized, Colum has become so adept with anapests he is sometimes able to use them successfully in rather unusual circumstances. Let us consider the poem, "Across the Door."

> *The fiddles were playing and playing,*
> *The couples were out on the floor;*
> *From converse and dancing he drew me,*
> *And across the door.*
>
> *Ah! strange were the dim, wide meadows,*
> *And strange was the cloud-strewn sky,*

And strange in the meadows and corncrakes,
And they making cry!

The hawthorn bloom was by us,
Around us the breath of the south—
White hawthorn, strange in the night-time—
His kiss on my mouth! (CP, *p.* 110)

The aura of wonder, occasioned by the abrupt change of scene from a gay, noisy dance to the unaccustomed quiet of the outdoors and emphasized by the refrain use of *strange* in stanza two and its repetition in the third stanza, is played off against the regularity and familiarity of the anapestic rhythm. The interruption of the regularity by the shortened fourth line surprises the reader in stanza three. The form, coupled with the key image of the virginal white hawthorns blooming in the night, reënforces the wonder of the girl's first kiss, as the poet, while seeming to let the events speak for themselves, artfully creates the scene and the moment.

The anapestic rhythm is also a staple of the poet's predominant verse form, the ballad stanza. Variations of the basic form are numerous but so well and subtly done as not to call attention to themselves. For example, the anapests in "A Connachtman" lengthen the first and third lines which are usually tetrameters, so that trimeters will suffice.

It's my fear that my wake won't be quiet,
Nor my wake house a silent place:
For who would keep back the hundreds
Who would touch my breast and my face? (CP, *p.* 86)

The rhyming second and fourth lines, which would normally be trimeters, are shortened by the substitution of an iamb for one anapest. The effect of the attenuated alternate lines is essentially that of the ballad stanza.

In "The Terrible Robber Men" Colum modifies the ballad stanza with the addition of an extra refrain line, another lyric device often found in his poetry.

Oh I wish the sun was bright in the sky,
And the fox was back in his den O!

> *For always I'm hearing the passing by*
> *Of the terrible robber men O!*
> *Of the terrible robber men.* (CP, p. 100)

The last two lines and the last syllable of the second line
are repeated in the two succeeding stanzas, and the emphasis of the poem shifts from narrative to lyrical, as we
become preoccupied with its sounds rather than its story
line or content.

"The Terrible Robber Men" is exceptional in Colum's
poetry in its use of a refrain line appended to a ballad
stanza. However, there are several musical poems in
which refrain lines are repeated with variations. One
frequent device is of a type common in sea chanties, a
modified repetition of the penultimate phrase to con-
clude each stanza. There is an example of this in "Hired
Scythesman."

> *For scythe must sweep from hedge to hedge to win the*
> *spalpeen's pay.*
> *From hedge to hedge, and quick at that,*
> *To win the spalpeen's pay.* (PC, p. 38)

Another variation of the refrain line technique is
found in "A Ballad Maker" where the repeated lines
(set off in the poem) are interspersed with two rhyming lines to form a caesura at the end of the first quatrain
and then provide a tag line on the tercet forming the
second segment of each stanza.

> *Once I loved a maiden fair,*
> Over the hills and far away,
> *Lands she had and lovers to spare,*
> Over the hills and far away.
> *And I was stooped and troubled sore,*
> *And my face was pale, and the coat I wore*
> *Was thin as my supper the night before*
> Over the hills and far away. (CP, p. 125)

The poem, a tale of lost love, is intentionally removed in
time and space from its narrator by the insertion of the
refrain lines, but their repetition fifteen times in the five
stanzas tends to become monotonous and blunt their
effectiveness.

Not all of the repetition in Colum's poems is so obvious, however; his most frequent use of the repeated line is in an unobtrusive reënforcement of an image, or in restating the initial proposition of a poem once that proposition has been modified by the rest of the poem. Typical of this refrain technique is the "cones of fire" image in "Laburnums."

> *Over old walls the Laburnums*
> *   hang cones of fire;*
> *Laburnums that grow out of old*
> *   mould in old gardens:*
>
> *Old maids and old men who have savings or pensions have*
> *Shuttered themselves in the pales of old gardens.*
>
> *The gardens grow wild; out of their mould the Laburnums*
> *Draw cones of fire.*
>
> *And we, who've no lindens, no palms, no cedars of Lebanon,*
> *Rejoice you have gardens with mould, old men and old*
> *   maids:*
>
> *The bare and the dusty streets have now the Laburnums,*
> *Have now cones of fire!* (CP, p. 188)

Here the "cones of fire" image contrasts with the grim surroundings and the old people, whose passionless, incapacitated existences are brightened by the colors. The passion of the cones of fire becomes more and more significant as the relationship of the cones to their surroundings is more clearly understood. In this poem the sight image as refrain is not isolated but acts as a modifier affecting the meaning of the rest of the poem by its presence.

Occasionally lines are repeated so skillfully and unobtrusively that one is not even immediately aware of the repetition. Half of the twelve lines of "Ishmael the Archer" are duplications.

> *Tomorrow I will bend the bow:*
> *My soul shall have her mark again,*
> *My bosom feel the archer's strain.*
> *No longer pacing to and fro*

With idle hands and listless brain:
As goes the arrow, forth I go.
My soul shall have her mark again,
My bosom feel the archer's strain:
Tomorrow I will bend the bow.
  —Spoke Ishmael son of Hagar so
  When he had mourned her on the plain,
  And all was left him was his bow. (PC, *p. 56*)

The repetition, instead of becoming tedious, works admirably in this poem rhymed only on two sounds, the onomatopoetic "Oh" sound of lamentation and the "ain" sound suggesting pain. Ishmael's suffering, then, is embodied in the sounds of the poem as well as its meaning.

Another typical Colum rhyme scheme is the quatrain stanza with alternating masculine and feminine endings. In such poems as "Egan O'Rahilly's Vision," the second and fourth lines are occasionally rhymed—though the regularity of the heavily accented last foot carries the burden of uniformity in others such as "At the fore of the year," so that the latter poem appears to be rhymed even though it is not.

With the exceptions of the dialogue poems and autobiographical narrative pieces the poetry is usually consistent in regular accentuation patterns and predictable rhymes. To be any other way the structure of the poetry would be inconsistent with the simplicity of its imagery and subject matter.

Simplicity must not be confused with lack of craftsmanship in Colum's images any more than in his prosodic techniques. Most of his poems are fairly short pieces defining a particular feeling or state of mind. One of his favorite techniques is a single image poem extended to an analogy to human behavior. These single-image poems are some of the most memorable of his canon. "No Child" is one of the most successful of this type.

I heard in the night the pigeons
Stirring within their nest:

> *The wild pigeons' stir was tender,*
> *Like a child's hand at the breast.*
>
> *I cried "O stir no more!*
> *(My breast was touched with tears).*
> *O pigeons, make no stir—*
> *A childless woman hears."* (CP, *p.* 114)

Because the speaker is so acutely aware of the significance of the simile, she draws the reader into an increased sensitivity to the analogy and its tremendous effect on her. As the reader supplies pathos for the woman's trauma, he also becomes just as convinced of the power of the pigeon image as she herself is.

In "Aquarium Fish" the leaf image is used like a refrain line, first expanding the consideration of the fish into the macrocosm of creation and later returning it to the microcosmic aquarium.

> *Mould-coloured like the leaf long fallen from*
> *The autumn branch, he rises now, the Fish.*
> *The cold eyes of the gannets see their rock:*
> *He has No-whither. Who was it marked*
> *Earth from the waters? Who*
> *Divided space into such lines for us,*
> *Giving men To and Fro, not Up and Down?*
> *This dweller in the ancient element*
> *Knows Space's cross-road. Who*
> *Closed up the Depth to us? He rises now*
> *Mould-coloured like the leaf long fallen from*
> *The autumn branch, with eyes that are like lamps*
> *Magicians fill with oils from dead men ta'en,*
> *Most rootless of all beings, the Fish.* (CP, *p.* 173)

The vertical-horizontal patterns of the motion in the poem are established by contrasting the fish's rising like a fallen leaf and the to-fro motion of men over the earth. Finally another dimension is accorded the motion theme by the last brief simile of the sinister aspect of rootlessness which living man avoids in the narrow confines allotted to him. As the refrain line brings us back to the original image and the fish, we feel a strange compassion for his lack of restraint and its concomitant living death which the poem suggests.

Colum is also master of the brief, visually descriptive image which makes no pretense at offering more than a precise summation of the essence of the way a thing looks. The monkeys in the poem of the same name are described as,

> Two little creatures
> With faces the size of
> A pair of pennies. (CP, p. 169)

Occasionally the poet's humor creeps into his visual images as he describes dancing Hawaiian girls as having "Bellies like millstones turning." (CP, p. 147)

The conceits in Colum's poetry are few, however, and the images, while not ingenious enough to call attention to themselves, are economical, honest, and rarely inappropriate. The structure of the poetry and the images reflect no great innovations; the poet has gone back to the most ancient verse forms, describing the appearance of things which are basically changeless in man and nature in readily understandable images which come from the same ancient catalogue. The result is a feeling of elemental antiquity in the poems.

Colum's poetry is best known for his characterization and dramatic lyrics. This popular judgment is well founded. Mr. Colum tells us:

My early training as a writer was in the theatre, and so when, after juvenilia, I began to write publishable verse, what I produced took the form of dramatic lyrics, poems arising out of character and situations—"A Drover," "A Poor Scholar," "An Old Woman of the Roads." . . . Dramatic lyrics imply succession: if this character and this situation are projected, why not other characters and other situations? And so, the theatre being back of me, it was inevitable that I should continue the writing of dramatic lyrics. After some decades of such writing I found I had enough poems of a particular kind to make a representative showing of persons and situations in an Irish countryside. (PC, p. v)

The Poet's Circuits is structured chiefly around these characterization poems, which comprise some of the poet's most notable works. Besides the poems mentioned in Colum's statement above, the portraits of the old soldier, the toy shop owner and the honey seller are among his best. Often, in the shorter monologue and dialogue poetry, his characters, in the tradition of "My Last Duchess," unintentionally betray the truth about themselves in their speech. The characterization, however, tends to categorize people with idiosyncrasies appropriate to a specific group rather than singling them out as individuals; so that Colum's shuiler (an itinerant homeless person who claims a night's shelter in a house) is preoccupied with getting "the good red gold" to buy herself a house (CP, p. 92); and the poverty stricken young woman of "The Poor Girl's Meditation" laments her lack of cows, sheep, and "the lad that I love for my own." (CP, p. 117)

In the poem, "Old Men Complaining," (CP, p. 60) the complaints of the three old men are typical of those of an easily recognizable class of aged, disillusioned, cantankerous men. The reader does not marvel at the unique qualities of any of the three, but has his already established ideas of the type reconfirmed by what the men say in the poem. The poem satisfies the reader because it strikes in him a responsive, if subliminal, chord of impatience with the prototype, so that the concluding righteous statement by the poet echoes the sentiment of the reader as well.

> *I heard them speak—*
> *The old men heavy on the sod,*
> *Letting their angers come*
> *Between them and the thought of God!* (CP, p. 62)

In one of Colum's most successful poems, "Scanderberg," the poet's visions of the pageant of history emblazoned in the epitaph of a tombstone are contrasted with the one line of dialogue uttered by a girl accompanying the persona. As she dangles her silk stockinged legs over the wall she refuses to proceed through the nettles around the gravestone, saying "I'll not have them [the legs] stung for any old man who is dead." (CP, p. 71) The line is sufficient to cast her in the same mold as Maugham's Mildred in the reader's mind as well as the persona's. The persona reiterates the statement as a prelude to a long enumeration of battles and days of glory and heroism.

In "Spadesmen," a dialogue poem introducing the "People on the Road" section of *Poet's Circuits*, we see the travelers along the road characterized by the spadesman according to their professions or groups. As the spadesman utters sweeping generalities to categorize people, he indirectly categorizes himself and his group. The following is the spadesman's statement about tinkers.

> *They have no friendliness for field or house.*
> *They have a curse for all who own a roof.* (PC, *p.* 117)

By this we see not only the spadesman's love for the fields, but also that despite the fact that he is in a sense an itinerant worker, he wants to put down roots and own his home. Though there is only one spadesman in the poem, the categorization process is made manifest in the plural title.

Occasionally the character portraits border on sentimentality, but the poet manages in most cases to stop short of debilitating excess. The portrait in "Old Woman Selling Ducks" is a pathetic picture of the woman forced to sell her bedraggled, scrawny, beloved pets; but, given the situation with its built-in pathos, the poet manages to avoid an overdose of sentiment in the last stanza by shifting the focus of attention to the fears of the ducks and the old woman as she trudges to the market to sell the birds.

> *From each end of the basket, too frightened to quack,*
> *A duck sticks a beak,*
> *And frightened is she, the old body who'd sell them,*
> *And hardly will speak:*

As she trudges along with her ducks, each as thin
As the water-hen! (PC, p. 87)

Not all of the character poetry is pathetic, however.
"The Call for the Bride" (PC, p. 102) is the dramatic
dialogue of a mother outraged when suitors call for her
daughter, and doubly outraged when her girl shows every
indication of willingness to go, even requesting a sizeable
dowry. Apparently giving up on her older daughter, she
shifts attention to the younger, vowing that the latter
will not go the same way. The mother's reluctance to let
her daughters go off, her protestations of the older
daughter's innocence, and her pragmatic immediate shift
of attention to her younger girl once the fight for the
older is lost, are genuinely funny. Colum says of the
poem:

> Indeed it is very humorous. I started to write it first for
> John McCormack and it is to the very jolly air called
> "The Balally Farmer." It is a number in the musical
> version of the *Road Round Ireland*. It was a great success.
> Both daughters want to go.[6]

The poet does not stop with human characterization
but applies the technique of dealing in prototypes to
other creatures as well. Practically all of Colum's portraits of birds and animals are rendered in the same
terms used to characterize humans: the jackdraws (CP, p.
154) are described as vagrants and the vultures as "im-
pure," sitting "in evil state," with "Raw marks upon
their breasts / As on men's wearing chains." (CP, p.
179) Hornets too are sinister creatures, "wary" and
"weaponed," whose nests are made like skulls.

Appropriately the poet comes closest to humanizing
the animals in "Monkeys." As the monkeys sit in the pet
store their loneliness is that of mankind.

> *There are no people*
> *To gape at them now,*
> *For people are loth to*
> *Peer in the dimness;*

> *Have they not builded*
> *Streets and playhouses,*
> *Sky-signs and bars,*
> *To lose the loneliness*
> *Shaking the hearts*
> *Of the two little Monkeys?*
>
> *Yes. But who watches*
> *The penny-small faces*
> *Can hear the voices:*
> *"Ah, do not leave me;*
> *Suck I will give you,*
> *Warmth and clasping,*
> *And if you slip from*
> *This beam I can never*
> *Find you again."*
>
> *Dim is the evening,*
> *And chill is the weather;*
> *There, drawn from their coloured*
> *Hemisphere,*
> *The apes lilliputian*
> *With faces the size of*
> *A pair of pennies,*
> *And voices as low as*
> *The flow of my blood.* (CP, p. 169–70)

Here the analogy is not implied but made explicit in the final line.

Other analogies between beasts and men are more ambiguous, such as the one in the fairly long narrative, "Asses," a poem about the grandeur of this commonly debased animal. After a beginning which describes the degradation of the species, the poet comes upon two creatures, proud, upright and tall, which are not cheap or mean but magnificent. This poem, stressing the attitude and greatness of the asses when they are treated with the dignity they deserve instead of being continually humbled, could easily be read as an allegory of the Irish race and nation.

When the poet delves more deeply into drama than mere lines of monologue or dialogue, he runs into trouble. His brief verse play "The Miracle of the Corn" is weakened by the all too evident attempt at symbolism. Since the days of Bunyan it has been exceptionally difficult to deal successfully with heavy-handed religious metaphors. In the stage directions of "The Miracle of the Corn," we are bluntly told that the corn is "the symbol of fertility." The poet fails to bring the play off because its simplicity and directness do not mix with the symbolism so obviously intended. As Sheila, the wife of a wealthy farmer, gives her husband's corn to feed the poor, his stock is replenished and he becomes wealthier. Sheila, through her role as the source of beneficence and fruitfulness, ultimately becomes the virgin-fertility figure. The play has lost some of its naïve innocence in its attempt at indirectness, but has not redeemed itself because the symbolism and the motives are so patently obvious. Except perhaps as an attempt at an Irish morality play, the piece carries little in the way of reader response.

"Swift's Pastoral," another short verse drama, is, on the other hand, quite successful. In the poem Swift indirectly tells Esther Vanhomrigh (Vanessa) of his relationship with Stella. The symbolism of the work is thinly veiled, but because of the blend of historical fact and the whimsy of Swift's own narrative point of view with its subsequent revelations of his character, the poem is more interesting than "The Miracle of the Corn."

It is indicative of Colum's humility that he never feels his poems are inviolable or incapable of improvement. He unhesitatingly changes not only finished manuscripts prior to publication but reworks published poems to fit into new schemes for subsequent volumes or merely to improve the poetry. For his most recent extensive collection of poems, *Poet's Circuits*, for Oxford University Press (1960), he rewrote a number of his earlier poems to fit into the medieval concept of the traveling poet and his circuits or rounds. The plan worked well and the context in which the poems appeared added even greater significance to some of his best work.

On occasion changes were made in the cause of clarity as well as unity. The poem "Polonius and the Ballad Singers" becomes merely "Singer," an introduction to the first of the poet's circuits, and the transformation results in a happy clarification of the narrative line in the earlier poem, especially in the elimination of the ambiguous "Polonius" of the earlier poem. The songs of the singers remain unchanged but the narrative linkage between the songs is drastically altered to provide a much clearer story line.

"Folding Hour" underwent a twofold transformation from its original rendition in an early volume, *Wild Earth*. The last stanza of the poem is as follows:

> *See the moon-cradle's rocking and rocking,*
> *Where a cloud and a cloud go by,*
> *Silently rocking and rocking,*
> *The moon-cradle out in the sky.*[7]

The stanza becomes semi-autonomous in the *Collected Poems* as it forms a prelude to a narrative poem called "The Ballad of Downal Baun." The latter poem is about a man who sets out to find a lost treasure and succeeds in gaining fortune by dint of his own toil and the help of a mysterious woman on a white horse. The connection between the poem and the "moon cradle" quatrain is ambiguous except for the night-time-anything-can-happen mystery it suggests. When the "moon cradle" stanza reappears in *Poet's Circuits* it occurs as the introductory and penultimate stanzas in the original "Folding Hour" poem, this time with a new final stanza. Once it is restored to its original context as a device to set a general scene of the sights and sounds of evening, it becomes again an integral working part of the poem.

Occasionally the poet unabashedly changes the poetry in tone as well as meaning to fit the context of a new situation. The first section of the two part "Furrow and the Hearth" becomes in *Poet's Circuits* merely a portrait of a sower. Let us compare the two versions of the poem:

Stride the hill, Sower,	*Stride the hill, Sower,*
Up to the sky ridge,	*Up to the sky-ridge,*

Flinging the seed,   *Casting the seed*
Scattering, exultant!   *While silence holds houses!*
Mouthing great rhythms
To the long sea-beats
On the wide shore, behind
The ridge of the hillside.

Below in the darkness—   *Below in the darkness,*
The slumber of mothers,   *The slumbers of mothers,*
The cradles at rest,   *The cradles at rest,*
The fire-seed sleeping   *The fire-seed sleeping*
Deep in white ashes!   *Deep in white ashes.*

Give to darkness and sleep,
O Sower, O Seer!
Give me to the earth—
With the seed I would enter!
Oh, the growth through the
    silence
From strength to new strength;
Then the strong bursting forth *And you casting the seed*
Against primal forces,   *As on mornings unmemoried,*
To laugh in the sunshine,   *Up to the sky-ridge,*
To gladden the world!   *MacCeacht or MacGrian!*
  (CP, p. 81)   *(PC, p. 38)*

In the first poem the portrait of the sower exists not as
an end in itself but rather as a means of strength and
inspiration to the poet. The sower is pictured "flinging"
the seed, "exultant" and singing loud songs as he works.
In the second poem the sower's "flinging" is toned down
to "casting," and he is not nearly so noisy about his
work. The contrasting silence of stanza two with its
hushed "s" sounds is introduced in the second version
even more succinctly and strikingly in the fourth line of
stanza one. Also, in the second poem we find that the
intimation is that the sower is up and sowing at an
unusually early hour, rather than flinging the seeds with
carefree abandon into the face of a primeval night. The
moral drawn by the poet in the first poem is lacking in
the second, where the sower is seen as a traditional
agrarian personage fitting a traditional role rather than
as a source of defiance and strength. While the second

poem is not so powerful as the first, it fits more closely the aim of *Poet's Circuits*, which is to rekindle memories of common things rather than to make bold new statements of freedom and exultation.

While most of Colum's changes in subsequent publications of his poems are judiciously made, a few appear unfortunate in terms of decreasing the effectiveness of the poems involved. One example of this is the poem "Girls Spinning" which, as it appears in both the *Collected Poems* and *Poet's Circuits*, consists of a kind of operatic dialogue between two girls who are considering prospective mates for the first girl. In the original version the girls listen to the songs of three suitors: the first, embittered and footloose after a betrayal by his previous lover, the second a bit overamorous, and the third a potentially devoted type. Of course the last is chosen. When the poem appears in *Poet's Circuits*, the first prospective lover's song is omitted, narrowing the choice considerably, and another poem, "Young Girl: Achill," from *Wild Earth* (WE, p. 20) is arbitrarily added to the end. While the addition is a lovely ballad sung by a girl who will kill herself if her lover does not come for her, its presence in the other poem disrupts the continuity and the story line.

While the poet does not hesitate to change his work if he feels it warranted in any subsequent publication, the most extensive changes were made to accompany the format of *The Poet's Circuits*, and there were few changes which were made ill advisedly in producing the volume which I feel to be Colum's best collection.

If Padraic Colum's principal poetic technique is lyric, the content of his poetry can best be described as romantic. He is preoccupied with such romantic subjects as the remote, the ancient, the supernatural, the pathetic, the exiled and the passionate. Because he is an Irish romantic poet, he is inescapably concerned also with nationalism and elegiac veneration of Irish heroes. His love of nature and all living creatures is still another aspect of his romanticism. Yet for all the passionate intensity his subjects would seem to provide, they are all made to seem familiar, natural and unpretentious.

Colum's penchant for things and stories of ancient times and remote places was destined to build an international reputation for him as a legend collector and folklorist. It is really only a short step from his ballads and folk poems to the legends of antiquity, and his poems constantly reflect this kinship between the past and present. The ease with which the transition is made is the subject of one of the "Reminiscence" poems.

It would not be far for us two to go back to the age of bronze:
Then you were a king's daughter, your father had curraghs on hore,
A herd of horses, good tillage upon the face of four hills,
And clumps of cattle beyond them where rough-browed men showed their spears.

And I was good at the bow, but had no men, no herds,
And your father would have bestowed you in a while on some unrenowned
Ulysses, or on the old king to whom they afterwards raised
Three stones as high as the elk's head (this cromlech, maybe, where we sit). (CP, p. 14–15)

In an ancient land, surrounded by the monuments of antiquity which stand as ever constant reminders of the past, the poet lives in an atmosphere in which the present and history become one indivisible continuum. Colum captures this blend of memory and present existence in his "At Cashel."

> *Above me stand, worn from their ancient use,*
> *The King's, the Bishop's, and the Warrior's house,*
> *Quiet as folds upon a grassy knoll:*
> *Stark-grey they stand, wall joined to ancient wall,*
> *Chapel, and Castle, and Cathedral.*
>
> *It is not they are old, but stone by stone*
> *Into another lifetime they have grown,*
> *The life of memories an old man has:*
> *They dream upon what things have come to pass,*
> *And know that stones grow friendly with the grass.*
>   (CP, p. 191)

As the present recedes into antiquity, facts and fantasy commingle to become legend and story. Colum knows, understands and writes about the area midway between fact and fancy, the immediate and the past, while his reader, who begins by asking, "What is fact here and what is imagination?" slowly realizes that it really doesn't make any difference; another chronological entity has been created, or more correct, utilized by the artist. Much of the charm of Colum's poetry and children's stories lies in the tantalizing ring of truth in his legends and in the unexpected apocryphal in what seems to be realistic. The transformation of realism to whimsy is caught in the second stanza of the poem "Legend." In stanza one the hour when dreams become realities is described. In the second stanza we learn of the dreamers and how they too become legends.

> A herd-boy in the rain
> Who looked o'er stony fields;
> A young man in a street,
> When fife and drum went by,
> Making the sunlight shrill;
> A girl in a lane,
> When the long June twilight
> Made friendly far-off things,
> Had watch upon the hour:
> The dooms they met are in
> The song my grand-dam sings. (CP, p. 136)

Dreams, songs, and the people who dream and sing them are for the poet parts of one continuous pattern.

Another reflection of Colum's feeling for antiquity is a profound respect for scholarship. Some of this is apparent in one of his most successful poems, "The Scribe." The poem deals with the making of an illuminated ecclesiastical manuscript, and its imagery catches the durability and sense of priceless historical importance which the document assumes.

> First, make a letter like a monument—
> An upright like the fast-held hewn stone

Immovable, and half-rimming it
The strength of Behemoth his neck-bone,
And underneath that yoke, a staff, a rood
Of no less hardness than the cedar wood. (PC, p. 60)

The act of creating the manuscript is the act of linking man with history, and the reader is made to feel the sense of profound importance in the scribe's work. Though the setting is the present, the aura of history permeates the poem and the reader feels that contemporary times are the ancient times of the future, that we are a part of antiquity.

Colum's romantic preoccupation with the remote relates not only to time but also to place. There are a number of Arabic love poems, Hawaiian songs, and poems of the mysterious East. Though the place and time of these poems may be removed from twentieth century Ireland, their stories and spirit might be those of County Cork. In "Kalmuck Bride" (CP, p. 133), for instance, the exotic daughter of the Khan admonishes her lover in the traditional fashion, telling him that while he is away on a conquering spree he should look at the moon and thus be vicariously united with her as she looks at the moon back home. Except for a reference to scimitars, the poem might have taken place anywhere. The remoteness of the location serves only to increase the sentimental quality of the thought.

Even the homely swallow profits from a certain glamorization through Eastern similies in "Swallow."

> *He knows Queen Lab, her isle,*
> *And black, enormous Kaf,*
> *The Swallow, and "Allah"*
> > *He cries*

> *As into Giaour lands*
> *With Dervish faith and rite,*
> *Hueless, a Saracen,*
> > *He flies.*

> *Like scimitars his wings,*
> *And, all unluminous,*

Black, like a genie's thought,
          His eyes. (CP, p. 165)

Here the poet, instead of discovering a universal commonplace in an exotic setting, transforms what appears to be a commonplace thing, the swallow, into a dark eyed, scimitar-wielding Saracen. Colum combines the romantic qualities of both Coleridge and Wordsworth in being equally able to see the glory and wonder of the ordinary and to render ordinary the exotic and remote.

Another major romantic tendency in Colum's poetry is an underlying sense of the pathetic: of poverty and hopeless love, of past deeds and glories which can never be duplicated, and of old people hopelessly resigned and young people grown old before their time. Even the poems which are not essentially about a particular calamity have a gentle air of pathos about them. The Colum poem which is perhaps his best known, "An Old Woman of the Roads," fits this description.

Oh, to have a little house!
To own the hearth and stool and all!
The heaped-up sods upon the fire,
The pile of turf against the wall!

To have a clock with weights and chains
And pendulum swinging up and down,
A dresser filled with shining delph,
Speckled and white and blue and brown!

I could be busy all the day
Clearing and sweeping hearth and floor,
And fixing on their shelf again
My white and blue and speckled store!

I could be quiet there at night
Beside the fire and by myself,
Sure of a bed and loth to leave
The ticking clock and the shining delph!

Och! but I'm weary of mist and dark,
And roads where there's never a house nor bush,

> And tired I am of bog and road,
> And the crying wind and the lonesome hush!
>
> And I am praying to God on high,
> And I am praying to him night and day,
> For a little house, a house of my own—
> Out of the wind's and the rain's way. (CP, p. 90)

The reader realizes the poignancy of the woman's fervent plea all the more acutely because of the meager proportions of her request and because he senses that even this will not be granted. In enumerating the few objects she wants in life, we see clearly the enormity of all that has been denied her.

If the old yearn merely for shelter, the young want only companionship.

> I am a young girl;
> I live here alone:
> I write long letters
> But there is no one
>
> For me to send them to. My heart
> Teaches me loving words to use,
> But I can repeat them only
> In the garden, to the tall bamboos.
>
> Expectantly I stand beside the door. I raise
> The hanging mat. I,
> The letter folded, gaze out
> And see shadows of the passers-by.
>
> In the garden the fire-flies
> Quench and kindle their soft glow:
> I am one separated,
> But from whom I do not know. (CP, p. 150)

The despondency in the poem is not really tragic, for there has been no spectacular love affair, no lover's death or forsaken love; there is only a vacant sort of pity for something which has never even happened, a pity which is real and moving but not precisely definable, an attitude of lack of fulfillment and a heartsickness born of natural inclination rather than significant loss or cataclysm. Indeed, one of the striking qualities about this aura of sadness is again the universality of its causes: the poverty stricken old woman has no home, the young girl has no lover, and in "Garadh" (CP, p. 101) an old man laments his lost youth.

The theme of the irretrievability of the past is a major source of pathos. Perhaps Colum's most direct statement of the ultimate cause of this sense of tragedy occurs in "The Big House."

The crows still fly to that wood, and out of the wood she comes,
Carrying her load of sticks, a little less now than before,
Her strength being less; she bends as the hoar rush bends in the wind;
She will sit by the fire, in the smoke, her thoughts on root and the living branch no more.

The crows still fly to that wood, that wood that is sparse and gapped;
The last one left of the herd makes way by the lane to the stall,
Lowing distress as she goes; the great trees there are all down;
No fiddle sounds in the hut tonight, and a candle only gives light to the hall.

The trees are gapped and sparse, yet a sapling spreads on the joints
Of the wall, till the castle stones fall down into the moat:
The last one who minds that our race once stood as a spreading tree,
She goes, and thorns are bare, where the blackbird, his summer songs done, strokes one metal note. (PC, p. 138)

The tragedy lies in the decay of people, things, and finally the Irish race and civilization. Ultimately the poet's characters realize the hopelessness of a decaying way of life, history and race. This theme, found in a great deal of Irish poetry and music, is usually linked to the usurpation of the British and the ever-present humiliation and poverty of a conquered people. The mood of defeat hangs heavily upon the poetry as the poet seeks new ways to express it. The analogy between the Irish race and the deer in "The Deer of Ireland" is obvious.

> An old man said, "I saw
> The chief of the things that are gone;
> A stag with head held high,
> A doe, and a fawn;
>
> And they were the deer of Ireland
> That scorned to breed within bound:
> The last; they left no race
> Tame on a pleasure-ground.
>
> A stag, with his hide all rough
> With the dew, and a doe and a fawn;
> Nearby, on their track on the mountain,
> I watched them, two and one,
>
> Down to the Shannon going—
> Did its waters cease to flow
> When they passed, they that carried the swiftness
> And the pride of long ago?
>
> The last of the troop that had heard
> Finn's and Oscar's cry;
> A doe and a fawn, and before,
> A stag with head held high!" (PC, p. 137)

The deer like the heroes, the will, and the hope of Ireland—are gone, and the attitude of loss is proliferated throughout the poetry until even the beauty of the lilacs in "Lilac Blossoms" [8] is not celebrated but lamented because it is transitory.

I do not mean to imply that all of the poetry is sad or resigned. There are moments of passion, though admittedly few, to rival any in romanticism's *sturm und drang* movement. "Branding Foals" is a portrait of a man on fire with feeling for the girl whose horses he is branding. In stanza two he describes his emotion in unequivocal terms.

> Why do I look for fire to brand these foals?
> What do I need, when all within is fire?
> And lo, she comes, carrying the lighted coals
> And branding-tool—she who is my desire!
> What need have I for what is in her hands,

If I lay hand upon a hide it brands,
And grass, and trees, and shadows, all are fire! (CP, p. 138)

The poems with foreign settings often have young, idealized, sensual women in them. These provide a considerable contrast with the pure, virginal qualities of the Irish girls who adorn his poems. Like Leopold Bloom in Joyce's *Ulysses*, Colum often turns to the East and dark eyed voluptuousness when he wants to portray the more sensual side of the female nature. The essential purity of Irish womanhood is a subject about which Colum has few reservations.[9]

Like most Irish poets and romantic poets, Colum has written his share of poems of exile. His longest poem *Lowry Maen* combines folklore and antiquity with exile in a long narrative about a young prince who, after years of trial and planning, returns to his country at the head of a mighty alien army to recover his usurped throne. Some poems, like "Ishmael the Archer" (quoted earlier), glory in the pride and strength of the outcast, while others stress the loneliness and isolation of the exile. In "Song of Starlings" the birds and their chirping bring back poignant memories of home to the exiled persona.[10]

. . . we hear the starlings
As we have heard them often in other cities,
Around other cupolas, along other cornices,
In sunless parks bunched on the tops of trees,
And see around us bleak, monotonous fields
Our hearts must ever hold—theirs are these songs—
These are the songs that most touch us exiles! (CP, p. 193)

The subject is of course both Byronic and Irish. While the pain of being cut off is acute, there is usually admiration for the freedom and headstrong will of the exile. For Colum, being chained to one's house and way of life can be to pass one's existence in a perpetual bondage like that described in "The Knitters" where the knitters ply their task "For the ten thousandth time," and talk of nothing else "But what was told before." All that can be hoped for by those that remain at home is to repeat their "wonted toil . . . / With grace and in content." (CP, p. 98)

The appeal of the wild and unfettered is also made explicit in "Wild Ass," where the ass has spurned with his hooves "the tombs of Archaemenian kings." The last two stanzas are a hymn to freedom.

> *The wild horse from the herd is plucked*
> *To bear a saddle's weight;*
> *The boar is one keeps covert, and*
> *The wolf runs with a mate.*
>
> *But he's the solitary of space,*
> *Curbless and unbeguiled;*
> *The only being that bears a heart*
> *Not recreant to the wild.* (CP, p. 168)

For Colum, as for other Irish writers, the worship of freedom is in some measure a subliminal wish for Ireland's freedom and independence.

For an author whose earlier plays were in the nationalistic tradition, who was referred to from the very early days as a spokesman for the Irish people and peasantry, there are surprisingly few poems devoted to the didacticism and propaganda which were so prevalent in the patriotic pieces of Lady Gregory and Yeats.[11] Colum's poetry is, of course, better off for it. His closest approach to militancy occurs in the poem "Blades" when the blade grinder sings to a group of unhearing citizens who are frittering away their lives:

> *Unready and unforward men*
> *Who have no right to any lien*
> *On the gifts of Tubal Cain,*
> *The gifts of our father, Tubal Cain!* (CP, p. 69)

The admonition to arm expressed here is unique in Colum's extant poems.

Colum's elegies are, in a sense, his most nationalistic poems. If they lack militancy, they are no less indicative of national pride and patriotism. Veneration of departed heroes, while a universal trait, is a particularly Irish preoccupation, and Colum's elegies have been reprinted with additions in Dublin every two or three years since 1958. These poems are gaining considerable stature as an increasingly significant part of his work. They are described in the volume *Irish Elegies* as being less elegies than memorabilia, and indeed it is the quality of the poet's having known these men intimately as friends as well as great men of Ireland that has given many of the poems their personal charm and significance. John Yeats is remembered for a personal remark at dinner as well as his magnificent artistry, and the figure of James Joyce with yachtsman's cap selling books and drinking pints at Barney Kiernan's is mingled with the creation of Anna Livia Plurabelle. It is, of course, in the nature of Irishmen to eulogize people and things dead and gone and to become so caught up in their reverie as to exaggerate on occasion. Colum rarely submits to this temptation, and his principal deviation is, understandably enough, in the elegy of his close friend Arthur Griffith, who becomes Odysseus in the poem. We learn in the introduction to the elegies that they are written immediately upon hearing of the deaths of the people elegized, so that we expect them to be full of feeling and high sentence. Colum does not disappoint us, but blends his praise with the simplicity and directness which we have come to anticipate and respect.

Laments for the loss of freedom and hope are rarely attributed to British usurpation or any other single source in his poetry. The anger has mellowed into futility in many poems, but the questions of why the loss occurred and who made it occur, though not often overtly raised, underlie many of the poems of desolation and poverty. Occasionally, however, the questions are succinctly put. Such is the case in "On Not Hearing the Birds Sing." The first six stanzas describe a country barren of blackbirds and thrushes, and the poem closes with the following question:

> *What grim marauder made a spoil*
> *Of bird and nestling,*

And left to us the songless woods,
The songless fields of Eirinn? (PC, *p.* 137)

The question is implied in all of Colum's poems of desolation and despair.

The usurpation-freedom motif is a prominant feature in Colum's "creature" poems. Some creatures like "The Little Fox" and the pigeons are abused, pathetic figures much like their human counterparts. The freedom of these two species has been usurped so that the fox finds himself on a leash and the pigeons have been domesticated and poorly used. The Eastern motif again is utilized in describing the pigeons as harem slaves.

Odalisques, odalisques,
Treading the pavement
With feet pomegranate-stained:
We bartered for, bought you
Back in the years—
Ah, then we knew you,
Odalisques, odalisques,
Treading the pavement
With feet pomegranate-stained! (CP, *p.* 162)

The human wish for freedom is embodied in many of the animal poems. In "The Deer of Ireland," "Wild Asses," and "Otters" the animals represent the free spirit which is part of man but which he has not been permitted to exercise. In "Otters" man's wish for animal freedom is most explicitly stated:

I'll be an otter, and I'll let you swim
A mate beside me; . . .

Now we go
Back to our earth; we will tear and eat
Sea-smelling salmon: you will tell the cubs
I am the Booty-bringer: I am the Lord
Of the River—the deep, dark, full, and flowing River!
(CP, *p.* 157)

Humans and other creatures have more in common than a mere love of freedom.

As Herbert Howarth testifies in *The Irish Writers*,[12] the Messianic vision has long dominated a considerable portion of Irish thought and letters and this has become a part of the Irish Nationalistic canon. Several of Colum's poems take up the subject. The most direct of these Messianic poems is "Egan O'Rahilly's Vision" in which,

> . . . *"the flambeaux are lit*
> *For sake of the King who is now bound for Eirinn*
> *Who to Justice and Faith the Three Kingdoms will knit!"*
> (PC, p. 139)

The Messianic wish is not often so obvious, however. More often the wish is for a builder, someone who might rebuild the homes and the fortunes of the depressed. Such a wish is embedded in "Dreamer of the New Hearth."

> *He shall arise;*
> *He shall go forth alone,*
> *Lay stone on the earth*
> *And bring fire to stone.* (PC, p. 30)

For another solution to the problems of his characters the poet often turns to the supernatural. One striking facet of this is the ease and lack of self-consciousness with which Colum is able to introduce the supernatural and make it appear as natural as the realistic details and setting which surround it. (This, of course, is doubly true in Colum's stories and will be discussed later in that connection.) In Colum's poem, "The Charm," the strength of leadership and freedom sought by the people in their Messianic desires are found through supernatural means. The poem recreates the legend of charmed water, which when found by chance in a hollow stone can transfigure the finder who knows the ritual speech and actions into a tower of strength and leadership. The finder in this case has every confidence in the miraculous powers of the water.

> *I empty the stone; on the morrow*
> *I shall rise with spirit alive;*

> *Gallant amongst the gallant,*
> *I shall speak and lead and strive.* (CP, p. 99)

The effect of the miraculous manifestations often extends beyond men into plants, birds, and animals. Even the mundane swallows are told:

> *Not alien to ye are*
> *The powers of un-earthbound beings:*
> *Their curse ye would bring*
> *On our cotes, and our glebes, and our fields,*
> *If aught should befall*
> *The brood that is bred in the eaves.* (CP, p. 4)

In the poet's vision, a whimsical world peopled with legends, fantasies, and superhuman manifestations coexists with the realistic world. The new world is a fanciful one in which the hopes, fears and desires of his people might easily be realized. This world does not in the Platonic sense represent the truth about or provide a basis for the realistic world, but rather represents an escape from it.

Colum's religious poetry does not necessarily fit the framework of romanticism which I have outlined. However, it cannot in good conscience be omitted from this discussion. Although he is not essentially a didactic Christian poet, Colum is a devout Roman Catholic and his Catholicism is reflected in several poems, notably "David Ap Gwillam at the Mass of the Birds" (CP, p. 152) and "Verses for Alfeo Faggi's Stations of the Cross" (CP, p. 194), a poem on Christ's crucifixion. The latter describes each of the fourteen stations of the cross as they are sculptured in bronze in St. Thomas's Church in Chicago.

"Fuchsia Hedges in Connacht" indicates the extent to which Colum is aware of his religious devotion and Catholic upbringing. The purple of the hedges sparks the following response from the poet:

> *I think you came from some old Roman land—*
> *Most alien, but most Catholic are you:*

> Your *purple is the purple that enfolds*,
> In *Passion Week, the Shrine*,
> Your *scarlet is the scarlet of the wounds:*
> You *bring before our walls, before our doors*
> Lamps *of the Sanctuary.* (CP, *p. 190*)

The purity and grace of youth is the subject of "The Bird of Jesus" (CP, p. 44), while the religious experiences of the Dantesque journey of manhood are recounted in "The Wayfarer" (CP, p. 142). These poems, though traditional in attitude, give us some indication of the deep religious convictions which underlie the rest of the Colum canon; for the respect, sympathy and love for man which permeate his poems, and the ease with which Colum deals with the world as it appears to the eye and ear stem from an attitude which may best be described as religious.[13] Richard Loftus discusses this religious quality.

> His verse is, to be sure, religious and, more specifically, Roman Catholic, but it is not religious in the same sense that the poetry of MacDonagh, Pearse, and Plunkett, or, for that matter, the poetry of Yeats and A.E. may be described as religious. These poets attempt to express, in one way or another and with varying degrees of success, a kind of religious experience that is introspective and subjective, and they place emphasis upon what may be termed spiritual values as opposed to material values. Colum's religion, on the other hand, is objective, almost materialistic, and it is concerned almost exclusively with the outward signs of God's revealed truth and with the human acts of faith that affirm those signs.[14]

But the unadorned, direct truth of sight and feeling is what is expected of a poet of the common people, a poet whose subject and audience are the common people, and a poet who prefers to be known not as symbolist, or creator of ingenious prosody, but one who merely is content to be called poet. Colum might have had an analogy to himself in mind as he wrote the following about the basket weaver:

For if you find and bring material
From willow-pool or hazel-dell far-off,
And make a thing that is of shape and use
Without bystanders or the noise of tool,
You are not spoken of by man or woman.
"The basket-maker has no name," he said. (PC, *p.* 85)

3

Drama

Padraic Colum's long career as a dramatist includes three distinct periods or phases. The first of these comprises his contribution to the inception and formative years of the Irish Theatre. Indeed, Colum's early reputation was made as much on the basis of his theatrical achievements as on his poetry. His name was identified with the origins of the Abbey Theatre, and generous predictions of his eventual stature as one of the great dramatists of Europe were made on the basis of his early works. He was especially linked with Edward Martyn, John Millington Synge, Lennox Robinson and T. C. Murray[1] as developing the realistic-naturalistic theatre of Ireland. The attempts of Colum and Synge to capture realistically the speech and attitudes of real peasant people were among the chief innovations of the Irish stage.[2] But for all his early promise, Colum in 1910 was to write his last play for the Irish Theatre, and in 1913 Cornelius Weygandt was to say of him:

> As dramatist he is still more full of promise than of achievement, and to be a dramatist of promise after ten years of play writing is to be at a standstill.[3]

L. A. G. Strong omits altogether a discussion of Colum's plays in *Personal Remarks*, telling us only, "I am passing by the plays, accepting Colum's own unspoken verdict on them, the fact that he so soon decided to leave the stage alone."[4] However, Mr. Strong was not altogether correct in his assessment of Colum's attitude toward the stage, for the playwright was to begin a second cycle of plays in 1916.

This second period encompasses nearly forty years and five plays. While Colum's interest in the theatre did not die, it certainly suffered a remission of sorts. He did, however, return to his scripts from time to time and work at extensive revisions. One play was rewritten under five different titles. His dissatisfaction with his dramatic endeavors was not wholly without foundation, as we shall see in a more detailed discussion of the plays later in this chapter.

At age eighty Colum launched the third cycle of his dramatic career with a series of five one act plays in the Noh tradition. He has only recently completed this series, which is substantially different in approach and effect from his earlier dramatic works, yet which utilizes a number of the more successful motifs and techniques he used previously.

With this outline of the three major periods of Colum's dramatic writing as a frame of reference, I wish to examine his plays from the standpoint of the artistic and historical standards which each period has sought to impose on his work; for unlike his poetry, which is personal and consistent, the plays seem to have been written to widely diversified sets of criteria.

The plays Colum wrote for the Irish Theatre were historically his most important contribution to drama and earned for him the almost immediate reputation of being in the vanguard of the new Irish drama. We should be reminded that Colum became interested in the stage while he was still working in the Irish Railway Clearing House. He owed his introduction into the theatre to William and Frank Fay, from whom he learned the practicalities of stagecraft. He acted in the cast of some landmark performances, the first of which was AE's *Deirdre*, presented April 2, 1902, the same night as Yeats's *Cathleen ni Houlihan*. A. E. Malone calls this performance "the real beginning of the Irish National

Theatre." [5] Colum played the part of Buinne, with Maire T. Quinn as Deirdre. Colum also appeared in the cast of the first Irish National Theatre Society production, in Molesworth Hall. The performance consisted of Yeats's *The Hour Glass,* presented together with Lady Gregory's first play, *Twenty-five,* on March 14, 1903. His acting career included at least one other production with the Irish National Theatre, Yeats's *The King's Threshold* performed with Synge's *In the Shadow of the Glen* on October 8, 1903. *Broken Soil,* Colum's own first major dramatic work, was presented two months later.

The Fays' Irish National Dramatic Company, of which Colum was a part, was formally amalgamated with Yeats's contingent, the nucleus of the Irish Literary Theatre, on February 1, 1903 with the founding of the Irish National Theatre Society.[6] Colum acted in the first two performances under the auspices of the new society and wrote a play for the third. In 1904 Colum was one of the twenty members of the Irish National Theatre Company who signed the original letter of agreement with Miss Horniman for the establishment of a permanent theatre on Abbey Street.

Colum's first two major works for the Irish Theatre, *Broken Soil* and *The Land,* enjoyed more immediate popularity than other writers' plays which were later regarded as among the greatest works of dramatic literature in English. His Irish plays, like his poems, had wide appeal because they fulfilled the popular demands of the period. It would be profitable to examine briefly both the aesthetic and the audience requirements of the time since these latter were as much patriotic, political and national as they were artistic.

The most definitive statements of Abbey dramatic policies appear in its preliminary announcement and its statement, "Advice to Playwrights." The intent of the Irish Theatre was clearly defined in the former.

> The Irish Literary Drama will appeal rather to the intellect and spirit than to the senses. It will eventually, it is hoped, furnish a vehicle for the literary expression of

the national thought and ideals of Ireland such as has not hitherto been in existence.[7]

This insistence upon intellectualism, which came primarily from Yeats, was destined to make many of the Abbey plays masterpieces of literature. But the other aspect of the announcement—the Abbey as a vehicle for "national thought and ideals"—opened the door for Colum and others who were intimately acquainted with that element of the population which it was generally supposed was the untainted and essential Irishman, the Celtic peasant.

Ostensibly Colum's plays deal with particularly Irish problems, and their resolutions are the inevitable outcome of circumstances of life in turn-of-the-century Ireland. Few critics, however, have realized that the real significance of his plays is not necessarily limited to such narrow confines.

The aura of realism and verisimilitude that Synge and Colum were to create was an attempt to bring a naturalistic flavor to the predominantly idealistic, almost metaphysical, intellectualism of Yeats and AE.

Colum's naturalism lay in his representation of peasant classes and especially in his ability to reproduce their language accurately. His early training and affinity for folk tales and language were just as important in his drama as they were in his poetry. It is difficult to overstate the relevance of this ability to the Irish Theatre, since the original dramatic movement had at its core a revival of the ancient Irish legends and civilization and an abiding faith in the language of the rural population as the proper language of poetry.[8]

The critics are far from accord about the excellence of Colum's dialogue. Weygandt feels that Colum's dialogue is his weakest point, claiming that his characters say characteristic things, but that their dialogue lacks "life." [9] Colum's tendency, so apparent in the poetry, to make his characters prototypes rather than individuals with individual idiosyncrasies, operates again in his plays. Weygandt however, confuses the commonplace dialogue of Colum's characters with a lack of "life" or reality. Herbert Gorman comes close to the same mistake when he says Colum "has trouble with his dialogue and at times it is inert, a heavy language, wingless and commonplace." [10] Like the dialogue of many of Arthur Miller's plays, full of seemingly leaden yet artfully constructed clichés and the accurately captured, deliberately lifeless expressions of real people, the very accuracy of the playwright's ear leaves him open to attacks from the critics. Colum himself has consistently taken pride in the verisimilitude of his dialogue.

> Yeats, Lady Gregory, Synge, and all were doing it, but the truth of the matter is that I was the only one of the lot that knew what the real country speech sounded like. I wouldn't want to say a word against Synge's language, which is exquisite, very fine, but has no more to do with how people actually spoke than Oscar Wilde's dialogue in his comedies has to do with how people spoke in London drawing rooms in the eighteen-nineties. You might say I had the advantage of the disadvantages that Yeats and others didn't have—I was born in a workhouse and knew common speech from my birth. I always say I was born in a workhouse to make a romantic story; the fact is, my father was the master of a workhouse, which isn't *quite* so good, not being quite so bad.[11]

The accuracy of Colum's ear for peasant speech had far-reaching repercussions for the Irish stage. As Malone points out:

> [Colum's dialogue] . . . is without the rhythm of the Western peasant, but it is a poet's selection of the more pedestrian speech of the Irish Midlands. In point of fact the speech used by Colum is a very close approximation to the actual speech of the greater part of Ireland. His dialogue seldom suggests the poet, and it is his characterisation rather than his speech that indicates the poet behind the play. The speech and the situations given to the stage by Colum led to the flood of ready-made "peasant" plays which every one in Ireland seemed capable of writing.[12]

Another criticism inspired by Colum's realism is that he deals with national problems in Ireland, but offers no solution to these problems. This introduces a larger question, one which gave the Abbey Theatre its most dramatic off-stage moments, the whole matter of morality and didacticism in the theatre.

Yeats was, of course, opposed to the idea of using plays as vehicles for propaganda. His circular to would-be Abbey playwrights spells this out in some detail:

> A play to be suitable for performance at the Abbey should contain some criticism of life, founded on the experience or personal observation of the writer, or some vision of life, of Irish life by preference, important from its beauty or from some excellence of style; and this intellectual quality is not more necessary to tragedy than to the gayest comedy.
>
> We do not desire propagandistic plays, nor plays written mainly to serve some obvious moral purpose; for art seldom concerns itself with those interests or opinions that can be defended by argument, but with realities of emotion and character that become self-evident when made vivid to the imagination.[13]

Colum's three major plays of the period comply admirably with these guidelines. Superimposed upon the Abbey's dicta were the demands of a vocal segment of the public that the plays represent the Irish in the best possible light and that they demonstrate the universal sweetness and light of Irish people and thought. That Colum's plays do not consistently glorify the nation, and that they do not attempt to solve the myriad problems of that troubled country are marks of distinction rather than causes for reproach. Always at hand to threaten the integrity of attempts at nationalistic drama were zealots whose black and white vision of the world admitted only propaganda as art. Though the Abbey leaders turned to Irish material for their plays, and though their tastes were far removed from those which dominated the London stage at the time, still there was a cosmopolitanism of judgment and taste which would never admit the narrow parochialism of those patriots whose idea of art began and ended with the flag.[14] If Colum's Irish Theatre plays were not written to the glory of the Irish, they were nevertheless about Ireland and its people.

The role of realistic peasant dramatist attributed to Colum is only part of the picture, however. There is as much evidence of Ibsen's influence on Colum as there is on his friend, James Joyce. Colum writes in the dedication to *Thomas Muskerry* (1910) that he has set down "three characters that stood as first types in my human comedy, the peasant, the artist, the official, Murtagh Cosgar, Conn Hourican, Thomas Muskerry." [15] Colum's panorama of character types and the truth about their social situations is pure Ibsen, as is his treatment of many characters. Colum's discovery of Ibsen had come quite early in life. In a piece entitled "Ibsen and National Drama," published in *Sinn Fein*, June 2, 1906, Colum writes of the analogous situations of Norway and Ireland, their demand for a national drama, and how in Norway Ibsen filled the need with his realistic characters. Colum might well have been discussing himself when he concluded:

> There is in Ireland a great feeling for character, not character as the modern novelists conceive it, mere psychological material, but for character living, breathing, moving—in a word acting. There is too a real aptitude for dialogue; newspapers and drawingroom conversation have not taken colour out of speech made by peasants and workpeople.[16]

The problems of Colum's Irish plays, like the dialogue, were real and the solutions to these problems neither clear-cut nor contrived. Because in *Broken Soil* and *The Land* the situations were readily understandable, realistic, and Irish, and because there was little to offend the parochialism of even the most militant would-be censors, Colum's first major plays were almost universally received as among the best of the Irish Theatre and Colum as the playwright with the greatest potential. Unfortunately Colum's potential was never fulfilled.

His early Irish plays which were full of promise were not the apprentice work of a great career but were instead the nearest he would come to drama of lasting literary consequence. The balance of this chapter will analyze his plays in an attempt to justify this evaluation.

Colum wrote six short dramatic pieces before his first full length play in the Irish Theatre. The first two, "The Children of Lir" and "Brian Boru," were published in *The Irish Independent*, and the next three pieces, "The Kingdom of the Young," "The Foleys," and "Eoghan's Wife," were all written and published in *The United Irishman* in 1902, before merciful obscurity descended upon the lot. The next year Griffith's paper published *The Saxon Shillin'*, Colum's prize winning one-act play which was later to cause such an uproar in the Irish National Theatre Society when William Fay refused to put it on. Colum says of *The Saxon Shillin'*:

> Willie Fay declined it on the ground that the main situation could not be staged effectively. But there were those in the Society who thought that his refusal to have anything to do with the production came from the fact that he did not want to have the garrison deployed against the hopeful theatre enterprise. There was a great row in which this person—at least in the eyes of Arthur Griffith, Maud Gonne and Mary Quinn—played a very weak part. The consequence was that Arthur Griffith and Maud Gonne withdrew from the Society. And so the link between the theatre and Cumann na nGaedeal was broken.[17]

The Saxon Shillin' was, however, subsequently produced on May 15, 1903. It is, considering the age and inexperience of its author, a fairly effective melodrama, relating the story of a young Irishman who has in desperation joined the British army (taken the Saxon Shillin') only to find that he is called upon to evict his own family from their home and to destroy it. He confronts his sister, at first defending his actions, but when he learns his father has been taken prisoner, and finds that his sister is left alone to protect the house, he remembers his

Irish heritage, picks up his father's gun, and marches out to be killed in a confrontation with the soldiers. The moral of the story, voiced in the line, "We can't buy ourselves back with the money we sold ourselves for," is ably demonstrated. Colum's career as a dramatist was to patriotic Irishmen, at least, off to an auspicious beginning.

The only other one-act plays Colum wrote for these early days of the Irish theatre were a children's play, "The Destruction of the Hostel," written for St. Enda's school and performed February 5, 1910; and a better-known work, *The Betrayal*. Colum wrote the latter for Arthur Sinclair to present under Abbey auspices, but it was first produced in Pittsburgh at the Carnegie Institute in 1914. *The Betrayal* found its way into Samuel French's catalogue and over the years has been put on in such widely diverse cities as Dublin, New York and Jerusalem.

The play is a melodrama set in Ireland and completely in the Irish tradition, with its themes of betrayal, the evil deeds of government agents and oppression. Briefly, the plot relates how two villains, one a town official, try to coerce an old ballad singer, who has come to plead for her deserter son's life, into betraying the murderer of an English solider. She steadfastly refuses, scorning threats of her son's execution and of her own physical harm and social ostracism, only to learn that the son has himself betrayed the murderer. Typical of its period, it relies for meaning on a comparison of the varying allegiances of the two generations, the older which would die before violating a trust, and the younger, all too willing.

The first major production of a Colum play and indeed Colum's first attempt at a three act play was *Broken Soil*, produced by The Irish National Theatre Society on December 3, 1903, in Molesworth Hall. The play was more normally and typically Irish than anything ever presented by the theatre. Its author was a representative Irish Catholic writing about the life and environment in which he had been raised. Oliver St. John Gogarty's criticism of the play appeared in *The*

United Irishman: "The play is built on the catastrophe produced from circumstances arising out of the temperament, religion, and tradition peculiar to the Irish people." [18]

Broken Soil brought Colum into the Fay fold. Colum had sent parts of the manuscript to Maire Quinn, who thought it showed great promise. She recommended the play to William Fay and one evening introduced the two at a rehearsal of *Deirdre*. Fay has a lively recollection of Colum's piecemeal composition of *Broken Soil*.

> Colum was a clerk at the railway clearing house. Office hours were long, and he had but little time for literary work; but whenever the spirit moved him he just jotted down at odd moments a poem or a scrap of dialogue on the first bit of paper that came handy—the back of an invoice or an envelope or the corner of some useless document. A lot of the first script of *Broken Soil*, the play that he sent to Maire Quinn, arrived in that form. When we decided to make *Broken Soil* the chief item in our December programme, the ever-helpful Maire sorted out the scraps for us and had them typed, while Colum was finishing the play in the same casual fashion. He would come into the hall at Camden Street, either before or after rehearsal, and, coming up to my table, would empty his pockets of pieces of paper of all shapes and colours and sizes, saying, "I've got a lot more here, Will." Then he would begin to shuffle the pack. "Here's the first bit . . . no, that's a bit of Act II, and that's another bit of it." Then, taking, say, a blue triangular piece, "Ah, yes, here's the bit to follow where we left off last time. And this yellow bit is next. And then this on the back of the envelope." It took a deal of patience to get the jigsaw puzzle into shape, but he learned dramatic technique very quickly, and I think his playing with us helped him to understand very soon the limitations imposed by a stage and proscenium. [19]

The play was an immediate success; Fay tells us of its reception:

> *Broken Soil* . . . was rapturously received. For the first time in our country we had not only enthusiastic audi-

ences but an enthusiastic Press . . . all were agreed that at last the Irish National Theatre was delivering the genuine goods, that at last there was a playwright untainted either by the mystical notions that had made them dislike Yeats or the unblinking realism that had made them hate Synge.[20]

Broken Soil was later revised and retitled *The Fiddler's House*. (It is the revised version to which I shall allude in this chapter because it is the one currently in print and available to interested readers.) *The Fiddler's House* in its present form was produced by the Theatre of Ireland in the Rotunda in 1907 and subsequently by the Abbey, August 19, 1919. The revised version, written after *The Land*, Colum's second play, is far superior to the makeshift affair Fay describes, and since it shows a progression in theme and technique from *The Land*, I will reserve discussion of it until later in the chapter.

Colum's next play met with equal critical acclaim. *The Land*, produced in the Abbey Theatre on June 9, 1905, was in Colum's words, "The first popular success the Abbey Theatre had had," in part because of the enormous interest of its subject matter. Its cast was a balanced, complementary one, in the comic tradition, with a father, sister and brother in each of the two houses. The plot deals with farmers who at the end of the land war are finally able to buy their own farms. The scene is set about 1885 just after passage of the Land Purchase Act, which decreed that when the tenant and the landlord agreed on the purchase price, the state would advance the money to finance the transaction and would subsequently be repaid by annuities over a number of years. However, the "land war" required to bring about this reform was a long and often bloody conflict, and by the time it had been won by the generation of Murtagh Cosgar and Martin Douras (the fathers in the play), there were for the young people other equally tempting alternatives to land ownership in Ireland. Martin Douras had gone to jail in the contest over the land and Murtagh Cosgar had sacrificed the greatest part of his life in pursuit of ownership. But the land they gave so much for had lost its attraction for many of Ireland's best young people. Thus, the play's basic conflict, which is of great concern to its audience, is the question whether the children are by this time still interested in retaining land and their roots in Ireland or whether they should go off on an exotic quest to the cities, excitement and promise of America. Colum tells us about the play:

> The passion for the land that motivates the first play is not likely to be responded to in days when farms are being abandoned and when the men who knew the oppression of landlordism as Murtagh Cosgar and Martin Douras did are not to be met with in the flesh. If staged these days "The Land" would have to be played as an historical piece and for character parts. However another issue could give relevancy—the revolt of the young against parental possessiveness.[21]

But Colum is being too modest in his assertion that the dilemma is dated, whatever its relevance to the problems of Ireland's earlier generations. There is also the universal antithesis between identification with the roots and tradition which the soil represents and the attraction of adventure, fortune and the Protestant ethic. The theme is not uncommon in American literature, appearing in such works as *Beyond the Horizon* and *Death of a Salesman*, and is particularly applicable to contemporary society. Another important matter Colum treats is the revolt of the younger generation against the authority of the older, a theme Synge was to treat so skillfully in *The Playboy of the Western World*.

In *The Land* the arrangement of two couples, one to stay at home, the other to emigrate, seems inevitable from the outset. Perhaps this is the weakest aspect of the play. The cast is typed so conveniently that the end seems seldom in doubt. The chief interest of the play lies in one of the young couples, Matt Cosgar and Ellen Douras. Ellen loves Matt, but will not admit even to herself her great wanderlust and dislike for remaining on

the land while others leave; and Matt, feeling the exultation of his emancipation from his father, unconsciously
yearns for the enslavement of Ellen and marriage, as she
persuades him to leave the Cosgar farm for America.
These are the characters whose self-realizations and aspirations, despite their inevitable course of action, form
the substance of literary excellence in the play.

The problem is not merely that of being a farmer or
an adventurer, or of leaving a forsaken land for a promised land; it pertains also to changing attitudes of class
culture and consciousness, as the following excerpt indicates.

MATT   . . . I'm not good enough for you. The people you
    know are better.
ELLEN   You are foolish to be talking like that. You are
    foolish, I say.
MATT   I know I am foolish. Fit only to be working in
    drains and ditches in the winter. That's what you think.
ELLEN   Maybe it is.
MATT   Ellen Douras! Ellen Douras! A farmer's roof will
    be high enough for you some day.
ELLEN   May I never see the day. Go back, go back. Make
    it up with your father. Your father will be glad of a
    labourer.[22]

Ellen's superior education may well have provided her
aspirations. There is a certain sense of objectivity in the
play which refuses to condemn her for these aspirations,
and this objectivity is one of the most attractive aspects
of the drama. The solution appears to have been scrupu-
lously impartial for that era with one couple leaving and
the other remaining. However, the character of the two
couples is vastly different. The stay-at-home couple, Sally
Cosgar and Cornelius Douras, are not as interesting dra-
matically, nor are they represented as being as vital and
alive as Matt and Ellen. Weygandt draws a moral from
this in his critique.

Matt and Ellen, the fit and the strong, go to America,
Cornelius and Sally, the hair-brained and the drudge,

remain. Symbolic this is, of course, of the situation in Ireland to-day, or at least yesterday.[23]

The play has a certain contrivance about its conclusion, but historically it is accurate regarding the migration of some and the triumphs of others who stayed behind. Ellen and Matt are nowhere depicted as being any more right in their decision than the remaining couple, who choose to "stay on the land and . . . be saved body and soul . . . saved in the man and the nation." Even this stirring sentiment at the conclusion of the play is somewhat mitigated by the ominous shaking of one father's head, so that the play does not attain a pat moral decision for or against either couple. Ellis-Fermore, discussing this point seems to find it a negative aspect of the play: "But the play is no thesis; it is a cross section of a living society . . . in which men do the right thing the wrong way and there is no plain, cut-and-dried issue." [24] However, it is the undercutting which leaves no character in the play unscathed or appearing to have all of the correct answers which is one of the best aspects of the drama, one which also is indicative of Colum's debt to Ibsen.

In many ways Colum's *Broken Soil* revision, *The Fiddler's House*, is much like *The Land*. The basic conflict arises again out of a choice between the romance of the roads and the shelter of a permanent home. In this play, however, the attractions of the soil are less apparent than in *The Land*. In both plays there are two ritual couples, but in *The Fiddler's House* the reconciliation of the first couple seems much less important to the conclusion, while the primary characters of the play, Maire and Brian, fail to achieve a blissful union, at least during the course of the drama.

Though the play's major problem seems to be whether the fiddler, Conn, should leave his house for the freedom of the roads, *The Fiddler's House* is really an examination of just what "freedom" constitutes. The dilemma is not Conn's. He has wanted from the beginning only the respect of those for whom he plays on the roads and the freedom of an itinerant fiddler's life. His statement that elsewhere there are people who know music and would appreciate him serves as a constant refrain in his speech, echoed even by the voice of the novice, Justin, who has been to other exotic climes (Salamanca, Spain) to study for the priesthood.

The Fiddler's House in its revised form makes fewer dramatic mistakes than *The Land,* especially in its greater subtlety of plot and characterization. The answers to the philosophical questions of the play are not readily apparent and even its resolution is left ambiguous. We know that one daughter will marry and remain on the farm, but there is no certainty that the other will ever marry. Though the old Fiddler will take to the roads again, whether his daughter Maire will do the same permanently or whether indeed, she even wants to do it, is left for the audience to conjecture.

The characterization, despite its freedom from stereotype, tends to reënforce the plot as an allegory of freedom. At one end of the spectrum there is Conn, whose sentiments are all for the open road, and at the other end there is James, described as somewhat arrogant at the outset, disposed to acquisitiveness and enchained by his grubbing, practical father. His mild rebellion from his father's yoke in the beginning of the play soon relapses into an acceptance of his father's ideas and ways.

In contrast Brian, the Byronesque, wild suitor of Maire, represents the freedom of rebellion against family ties and convention. He is a faintly sinister character who plans to carry off Maire until he yields to better judgment at the last minute. Conn's daughters, Ann and Maire, stand in varying relations to freedom. Ann's bondage is to her farm and James, and Maire's, for all her self-assertion, is to her father. The question of whether Maire really wants to take to the roads again is left unsettled. The itinerant life has attraction for her, but throughout the play she espouses a home in the village. When Brian offers her precisely that, however, she rejects him and refuses to consent to marry him or even to return to the locality once she leaves. The question we are led to ask is "Why?" Does she suspect Brian of being too wild and untrustworthy, or does she, like her father, really love the attractions and freedom of the roads?

The ambiguity of Brian's figure also poses some problems for the audience and enhances the value of the play. His wildness and dark appearance at first hold Heathcliff-like connotations, which then become Mephistophelian when Brian tempts Conn to the local tavern for an evening's fiddle playing, despite the fiddler's promises to his daughter not to go. Brian's call is one of freedom and lack of inhibition about which the play and the audience can make no conclusive moral judgment.

We are convinced that the road is the right place for the fiddler, for he is an artist demanding recognition he cannot receive at home. But we are not certain that it is desirable as a way of life for Maire. Whether Brian can accommodate himself on a local farm, no matter how splendid the house, is another matter left unresolved. Colum also employs the fiddler as a structural device, for we hear his music as a constant background underscoring the dilemma and playing a counterpoint against the action and speeches of the characters, a dramatic innovation for 1907.

The Fiddler's House, then, with all its similarities to *The Land* in characterization and dilemma, presents us with a much more sensitively portrayed and individualized set of characters, a more fluid and less obviously symmetrical plot, and some innovation of technique. Colum was making progress as a dramatist.

If the reception of *Broken Soil, The Fiddler's House*, and *The Land* was exceptionally favorable, Colum's last major play for the Irish stage, *Thomas Muskerry*,[25] had no such easy time among the critics. The storm over the play began with mixed reviews either ecstatically proclaiming Colum the greatest realist to appear on the European stage since Ibsen, or attacking him for defaming the character of his countrymen. Colum, like Synge, was assailed as portraying all the worst in the Irish peo-

ple when he might have shown them in a more favorable
light. The critical controversy went on for months in
Sinn Fein under a weekly column entitled, "Muskerry-
ism." When Colum was accused by "K." in the July 16,
1910 edition of fostering only a poor imitation of Ibsen,
he took up the gauntlet and wrote a scathing rebuttal in
the next issue. The tempest over *Muskerry* never reached
the proportions of the *Playboy* controversy, but three
years after the *Playboy*, the issues were the same, though
worn with the abrasive hand of critical repetition.

Thomas Muskerry is in many ways the most moving
of Colum's three early plays, perhaps because it is the
only tragedy. However, Muskerry's figure is pathetic
rather than tragic, for he undergoes no real conflict of
values. He begins the play as master of the Garrisowen
Workhouse and suffers gradual debasement until he finally dies a pauper in the institution he formerly ran. The
story is unusual in Colum's work for its uncompromising
analysis of man's meanness to his fellow human beings.
Muskerry has raised a daughter, Mrs. Crilly, whose only
care is for herself and her own family. Her daughter,
Anna, had inherited her mother's selfishness so that the
second and third Muskerry generations have developed a
callous disregard for their forebears. Muskerry and his
son-in-law, Croften Crilly, have each been cheated by a
scoundrel who has run off to America leaving them to
pay his debts and shortages. Muskerry is forced to resign
when his daughter refuses to return a previous gift of
money so that he may meet his shortage. Anna likewise
refuses her mother part of her promised dowry to pay off
the Crilly's debts, in a sort of allegorical round robin of
human greed. Muskerry seeks temporary refuge in the
workhouse, but when he tries to leave he is prevented by
James Scollard, Anna's new husband, and now the master. Scollard detains Muskerry on the insistence of Mrs.
Crilly, who feels that Muskerry's going to his own home
instead of the Crillys' would discredit her in the eyes of
the townspeople and that she would lose business in her
shop. Muskerry, defeated and discredited, dies of a

stroke in a pauper's bed in the workhouse.

Only in a small way is Muskerry responsible for his own problems. He has, of course, raised an ungrateful daughter. Seeing himself old and defeated, he also refuses a partnership in what promises to be a lucrative business.

> I'm an old man, Christy. And what does an old man do? He looks on and he looks back. Peter Macnabo is the same age as myself, but he's not an old man. I couldn't be with him.[26]

Muskerry, however, never has any major dilemma inside or outside himself which he must struggle to resolve. His role in the play is marked by a constant succession of defeats and never is the outcome anything but certain. To this extent the play is less than great tragedy. There are also certain incongruities which tend to mar the drama. For instance, why Crofton Crilly, a grubbing, selfish man, backed the note of a ne'er-do-well without material advantage is never explained.

What, then, are the redeeming features of the play? The figure of Muskerry is believable, even if a bit Dreiser-like, and his fall from master to pauper never quite degenerates into sentimentality. Somehow Colum has caught in this play the dignity of the aged and the poverty stricken in spite of their handicaps. Evidence of this dignity is shown in the proud piping of Myles Gorman, a pauper who returns to life and the road, and in the gentility of Christy Clarke, a pauper reared in the workhouse, whose humility is coupled with genuine ability and ambition.

The natural goodness and harmlessness of the workhouse paupers is perverted by Felix Tournour, the gatekeeper, who links the workhouse with the outside community and its attendant avarice. Tournour undermines the feeling of mutual trust and respect Muskerry has brought to the workhouse, and replaces it with the envy and avaricious ambition which dominate the attitudes of the community and Muskerry's tradesmen family. The

ambition of Tournour and others usurps everything that
Muskerry has tried to build, and in his fall we sense the
end of an era of natural kindness and dignity. It is this as
well as Muskerry's personal misfortune that brings real
pathos to the conclusion of the play.

Colum obviously writes the play from a position of
great familiarity with workhouse life and with the paupers who are its inmates. There is in Muskerry more than
a trace of the commanding presence and good-man-
brought-low tragedy of Colum's own father. Perhaps the
call of the road and America in the preceding two plays
is also a product of Patrick's image. At any rate *Thomas
Muskerry* reflects a more mature handling of characterization and stagecraft than its two predecessors and,
granted flaws in plot and motivation, is much more
meaningful drama.

With all that, however, the chief value of *Muskerry*,
and indeed the three plays comprising Colum's contribution to the Irish theatre, is less in their dramatic or
literary quality than in their sociological and historical
importance. They were the first of a kind of drama, and
as an evocation of a world gone and nearly forgotten,
even at the turn of the century, they presented the
hopes, misfortunes and even meannesses of a rural people who were remembered with hazy, blissful perspective
by the Irish of a nation on the eve of its independence.
The partisan audience in those early days of the Abbey
preferred to idealize their country folk, but Colum even
more than Synge was the one playwright whose pen
could accurately sketch such characters and make them
so authentic that the audience, whether it wanted to or
not, had to accept them. Constantine Curran has a vivid
recollection of Colum's contribution: "As students we
had the sense not only of something new or novel, but
genuinely Irish." [27] Muskerry himself provided an accurate appraisal of Colum's real value to the Irish theatre.

> When I walk out there and through the gate by the
> roadside it will be the same as if a history was ended. Do
> you know, Christy, when I came here there were old men

in the wards who had stood before Daniel O'Connell at Mullaghamast. They came from different parts to hear him that day. "Forty of us slept in the one bed," one of them said to me—"a ploughed field." That was history. And when I go out of the gate there will be something different here. Old Ireland will have gone out of it.[28]

After *Muskerry* the young playwright for whom those concerned with the Dublin stage held such high hopes was to wait nearly fifty years before writing another major play for an exclusively Irish audience. We can have no doubt, in the light of the improvements he made in each successive play, that there was a vast difference between the author of *The Saxon Shillin'* and that of *Thomas Muskerry*, but Colum still had much to learn before he could write enduring drama. Four years after *Muskerry*, however, he left Ireland for a new life in the United States, a new circle of acquaintances and an entirely new set of principles and ideas for playwriting. Each of his subsequent plays was an experiment with yet another set of dramatic criteria, as Colum searched for a suitable vehicle to release his ever present urge to write for the stage.

Colum's second major period as a dramatist, which extends through the 1950's, includes four plays. The first of these included in its original cast Orson Welles as Chosroes, the King of Persia. The play, like most of Colum's work, has undergone numerous changes, and at least four versions, *The Desert, Timbuktu, The Vizier,* and *Mogu the Wanderer,* have surfaced over the years. The last version, produced at the Gate Theatre in Dublin and published in book form by Macmillan in 1923, is the one at issue in the following discussion.

Mogu follows certain trends Colum pursued in his poetry. A segment of his poems treats the remote and exotic, most notably the Near East. This setting allows him a freer reign of imagination and subject matter than the social plays he had been writing. High romance and kingdoms lightly changing hands are not a normal part of plays about comtemporary Ireland. Thus *Mogu* provides the scene for such fairy-tale happenings as a beggar's rise to unprecedented power, and the love affairs of exotic, veiled women. This play is also the first of two unsuccessful attempts to make plays out of fairy tales. Some of the things which were to work admirably in Colum's children's stories were not the stuff of serious drama. Subsequent revisions beefed up the character of Mogu, making him more self-righteous and complex, but the early version lacked that. Although the play is graced by such touches of Colum's appreciation of the absurd as Mogu's reluctance to part with his nose as a love offering, it is for the most part, doomed as serious drama by weaknesses in motivation and character development. Yet there are too many serious actions, such as the murder of a king, to make it farcical. In its hybrid form it can only be considered an unsuccessful experiment in fairy tale drama.

Colum's next dramatic offering was *Grasshopper*, a free translation of a Keyserling play. E. Washburn Freund collaborated with Colum in the translation, and Colum, given the skeletal outline of plot, reworked the play. It was produced in the Abbey, October 24, 1922, but the text of the play was subsequently lost in an Abbey fire.

The fairy-tale motif appeared again in Colum's plays in 1929 when he embarked on an experiment in Strindbergean impressionism with *Balloon*. Again there have been many revisions of the play, the latest including new characters and themes. Since one version found its way into print (Macmillan, 1929), and this was substantially the same version produced in Ogunquit (see earlier reference in biography), it is to this version which I shall refer.

The play is essentially an updated version of *The Land* in its theme of the pursuit of the elusive carrot of success as contrasted with a return to the old ways and the slower pace of life in communication with nature. There is much of Colum, the fanciful, rustic poet, in the character of Glock, an old piper who now runs a nursery but who can't make children play as he used to. Glock's lamentation conveys the nostalgia for an older, simpler life, perhaps back in the Cavan hills.

> The children here are not as you might think they are; they are not like the children of our world, sir. They are not to be piped into playing, I assure you.[29]

The three main characters, Paras Veka, Caspar, and Glock are misplaced, Glock in an unfeeling world which has ceased to appreciate the natural life:

> I won't get any of them to go with me . . . to a place where there are Sundays . . . And settings for Sundays . . . Grass, of course; cows, a bird on a bush or a briar, or whatever it might be, bells ringing over the fields.[30]

The dilemmas of Caspar and Paras Veka, the protagonist and his prospective mate, are quite similar to Glock's, though suited to their respective sexes. Caspar is a poor vendor who longs for the glamorous world of the Hotel Dedalus across the street from the park where he works, while Paras Veka is, of course, looking for a husband, as are all good Irish-American-Polish girls. However, she would like a knight in armour since her values, like Caspar's, need refurbishing. In fairy-tale fashion they get their wish to participate in the life of the hotel as the play proceeds through a set of surrealistic adventures culminating with their discovery that the simple life is best, whereupon they return, together with Glock, to contemplating nature in the park.

Throughout the play we hear not only overtones of fairy tale situations and Strindbergean images, but also of Colum's friend, James Joyce. The Hotel Daedalus, the *Bildungsroman* situation, and the concluding speech of Caspar are all reminiscent of *A Portrait of the Artist*, though only in Caspar's speech is there any marked echo.[31] I am sure the borrowing from Joyce and other sources was less a conscious effort than an attempt to synthesize something new on the part of the dramatist. It was an effort to write for a new audience, vastly different from the crowd of partisan Irishmen back at the Molesworth Hall. The attempt was doomed, partly because the influences were blatantly apparent, and partly because the thin plot apart from the devices was too negligible a framework to drape in the heavy, ornate cloth of so many symbolic contrivances and images.

The false values of the Hotel Daedalus and its cosmopolitan atmosphere reflect some of Colum's sensibilities regarding the ephemeral values of his newly chosen land, and Caspar's return to the park is a reaffirmation of the old world of Ireland, the qualities of which form the basis of Colum's best work.

The last of the plays in this period of Colum's writing had again several titles. Originally called *Theodora*, it was revised in 1956–57 and retitled *The Bear Keeper's Daughter*. It was never produced, though excerpts from it were performed at the Irish Literary Society in New York by Jennie Egan.

The play, the first to be partially in verse, attempts to set Theodora, a former courtesan-actress turned noblewoman, as an all encompassing female principle. Her part is a riotous succession of mysterious wild passions and occult doings. During the course of the play she reverts to her cunning former self to uncover a plot against the empire and her husband to be, Justinian, the successor to the throne. There are testimonials throughout the drama to the many guises in which she appears: the innocent virgin, the dignified courtesan, the cunning wanton and the frenzied pagan. She is tormented by her desire to abandon herself to her former excesses, but at the end she seems finally freed from the passions of her youth. The character of Theodora is Colum's only effort to represent a complex, symbolic female principle and it is in the main a laudable attempt. In a sense the complexity of Theodora's character is parallel in part to the diversity of Christian and pagan attitudes that conjoin in her sensibility. Justinian's Christian forgiveness of Drimakos, who has wronged Theodora by accusing her in obscene pictures of murdering her former lover, is contrasted with Theodora's demand for revenge and punishment, a pagan attitude. But later her pagan characteristics serve her in good stead as she uncovers the plot for the overthrow of herself and Justinian. To complete the Christian versus pagan theme, the plot is led by a Christian zealot and prompted by a pagan Machiavellian.

Colum's play is loosely based on Procopius' account of the history of Theodora and Justinian, but with the popular uprising historically placed before Justinian assumes complete control over the empire. Some of the enigma and self-possession of the historical Theodora are indeed conveyed by the heroine of Colum's play, which lacks consistent character credibility more in the minor roles of Simon and Zero than in the major roles. The play is the only real history play attempted as such by the playwright, and on its own terms it is moderately successful.

In my opinion Colum's best dramatic work of the period was in the form of the scenario for a puppet cartoon of *Hansel and Gretal*. Colum and his wife were commissioned to do the work for a forthcoming picture by Michael Myerberg. The script was translated from Humperdinck's opera by Mary and freely adapted for the screen by Padraic. In *Hansel and Gretel* Colum comes into his own imaginative element. His fantasy world is peopled with dancing furniture and household pets (three bears and a duck), impish children and a sinister witch. The story is told in a straightforward manner with no question of confused motivations or characterizations. It really represents Colum at his lyrical, imaginative best, in which he is able to suspend verisimilitude and let his fancy have full sway.

Colum's last dramatic cycle consists of five one-act plays, three of which, *Monasterboice, Glendalough,* and *Cloughoughter* were produced in 1966 at the Lantern Theatre in Dublin under the title, *The Challengers.*

These last plays are all in the tradition of the Japanese Noh Theatre, a form utilized by Yeats in his cycle of Noh drama in 1915. According to Japanese custom the plays run in cycles of five, as do Colum's, but unlike

Colum's cycle the subject matter of the five successive plays is prescribed as being concerned with God, man, woman, frenzy, and devils. Other than their departure in theme, however, Colum adheres fairly closely to the dictates of the Japanese form: the plays are partly in verse; he peoples the stage with ghosts and choruses; there is usually a confessional scene; and his settings are associated with shrines. In the introductions to *Clough-oughter* and *Moytura* Colum sets out some of the Noh criteria which provided his models.

> In the Japanese Noh a place is central, and the legend that the place enshrines is the subject of the play. One of the main differences between the Noh and the plays of our theatre is in the time element: we proceed on a single level of time—it may be present time, it may be historic time. In the Noh play the action passes from level to level, from the contemporary to the historic, to the mythologi-cal. Certain characters wear masks; there are dances or ritualistic movements.[32]

> In our theatre we strive to bring the audience close to the action and the action close to the audience. In the Noh theatre a different effect is aimed at. The action is not brought close but put at a distance from the audience. It is made remote, but its emotional effect arises from the pathos of distance.[33]

The plays afford Colum another chance to free his fantasy from the realistic details of western drama, to probe the heart of ancient Ireland and to reminisce in blank verse. These last plays are statements of dramatic, historical situations, resplendent with beautiful language but without the necessity of effecting a resolution ac-cording to the dictates of formal plot structure. Unlike the Noh protagonists of the Japanese theatre, Colum's characters do not exorcise their demons; they merely state their problems. But the statement is made elo-quently and in most cases is sufficient.

In his cycle Colum peoples shrines of great antiquity with protagonists of more recent Irish history. Their personal dilemmas and crises are recounted in association with the settings.

Moytura, the first play in the series, deals with Sir William Wilde, the father of Oscar Wilde and a famous surgeon and antiquarian who made excavations at Moytura, the site of a prehistoric battle which according to Irish mythology originally was fought between the powers of darkness and light. Wilde, a ghost in the play, reënacts at the site his own personal struggle of receiving the news of the accidental death by fire of his two disowned illegitimate daughters. Two figures who form a chorus background describe the violent emotions of ancient warriors as Wilde's passions well up at the news. He addresses Nuada, one of the titans who preceded him, and finds strength and purpose in the words of the ancient king. As Wilde leaves, a young man whose search for Moytura provided the preliminary exposition of the play returns to pronounce history's judgment on Wilde. The epilogue does not seek to minimize Wilde's guilt and no real progress in terms of a normal plot line has been made. However, Ireland's distant past and its recent history begin to merge as one continuum, and the sense of living in history which one gets from visiting ancient sights is convincingly conveyed.

In *Glendalough* the playwright abandons the situation used in *Moytura* of a ghost protagonist. In *Glendalough* the protagonist is Parnell, who, following the O'Shea divorce, in which he was named correspondent, has come, on the eve of the meeting which will determine his rule over Irish politics, to the ancient site of St. Kevin's Church and medieval university, there to find the truth about himself. The history of Parnell's affairs and his nearly successful fight for home rule for Ireland are reviewed as he strives for self knowledge. The ghost of Pigott, the forger, rises up to tell Parnell that there is the forger in him also, and Parnell's mistake in appointing Captain O'Shea to a seat in Parliament forms another facet of the leader's self-evaluation.

Colum has cast the play in Glendalough because of

the historical affinity between Parnell's story and the
legend of the hag of Glendalough, whom St. Kevin,
"threw down the cliff and into a lake . . . Because she
would share his bed in the cave." The lust of a woman
has not brought St. Kevin low but it will Parnell. He
sums up his quest:

> I know myself now. And there are other things in Glen-
> dalough that have brought me to know myself. The one
> who called herself Kathleen! [the hag] [34]

Again the end of the protagonist's discovery of the truth
about himself is not accompanied by any decisive action
such as Oedipus putting out his eyes, but mere recognition is deemed sufficient.

Like the later plays in this series, *Glendalough* is written predominantly in prose rather than poetry. Despite
the ghosts there is much less fancy than historical detail,
so that prose would seem to be the proper medium. The
play recapitulates an important moment in time rather
than making a new statement about the event, as Colum's talents as historian and tale teller assert themselves
along with those of poet and fantasy writer.

Cloughoughter is set in the place where Owen Roe
O'Neill, the seventeenth century Irish general, died.
Roger Casement, the protagonist, has come to seek the
answers about whether he should assume the mantle of
Irish revolutionary leader. Against a lengthy background
of seventeenth-century Irish history, O'Neill's advice,
and the exhortations of two fugitive volunteers from the
battle of Kinsale, Casement, of course, decides for heroism. *Cloughoughter*, like *Glendalough*, is in prose and
full of historical fact. The structural variation in the play
consists of an epilogue in which Casement's brother,
Tom, returns to Cloughoughter after Casement's trial
and execution for treason, and hears his brother's deeds
in a ballad being sung throughout Ireland; the fame that
eluded O'Neill has thus been granted Casement. The
only disturbing thing about this device is that it mixes
four time-levels: Casement's time, O'Neill's time, the

time of the battle of Kinsale, and the time subsequent to Casement's death. Colum informs us in the introduction that this is part of the *donnée* of the Noh form, but it is not always easy to suspend sequential credibility in a history play dependent for its being on the sequence of historical fact.

Monasterboice, representing James Joyce's search for identity, takes place in the ancient monastery containing the Cross of Muirdeach, an elaborate ancient Celtic limestone symbol with figures representing the cycle of man's life carved on both front and back. Joyce's work, with its cyclical overtones, matches the cyclical mood of the place. The answer to Joyce's search lies not in Emma Clery, who accompanies him to Monasterboice, but in his *non serviam*, stated here and in *Portrait* as his credo. Emma, who goes by the initials EC in *Portrait* and her full name in *Stephen Hero*, is portrayed in *Monasterboice* as following Stephen's concept of her in *Portrait*, in which she represented for him the voice of the siren luring him back upon the rocks of the church. In Colum's play she fails to convince Joyce to return to the fold and so do the "emissaries," the Jesuitical voices which implore Joyce to join them. We are reminded that Joyce's work is irrevocably linked with Thomist theory and that his life has always been concerned with the church. Like Stephen Dedalus, Joyce rejects the entreaties of Emma to lead a respectable Irish life as her husband, and the entreaties of the monastic voice for a life of clerical celibacy. He goes off in the end with his father and a Mr. MacAnaspy for a "jollification" and the life of an exile.

Monasterboice covers a number of the problems central to Joyce's life and work, but not in a very convincing manner. Since there is neither the legendary heroism nor melodrama associated with the other protagonists of Colum's Noh plays, the character of Joyce must be viewed realistically, and the Noh play is a better vehicle for a stylized than a realistic appraisal of a man's life or problems.

The last play in the cycle and the last play Colum has written, completed in 1965, is *Kilmore*. It deals with the Ulster leader, Henry Joy McCracken, and is set in the place where Bishop Bedell offered his protection to Irish Catholic scholars. The joining of Irish Catholic and Protestant forces is reënacted once more in the rising of 1798, when McCracken attempts to unite the Ulster men with the rest of Catholic Ireland in the rebellion. More dramatic and realistic than the earlier plays in the cycle, *Kilmore* portrays McCracken's scheme for the rebellion, his near betrayal, and his final determination to carry through the revolt to "raise the spirits and pride of the Irish people," even though he knows that the French, upon whose help he had counted, will not come. Receiving the news of the refusal of the French to join in the rebellion, McCracken makes his decision at Kilmore to go on with the rising.

The play is not nearly so stylized a piece as the earlier four, and, while it has a few of the Noh trappings and the same general plan as the earlier plays, the action is real rather than pageant-like. It points up the fact that the plays in this cycle are considerably different from each other in scope, in intensity and in dramatic value. More than a series of "great moments in Irish history," or mere elegies, they attempt to establish a continuity between the ancient Ireland of legend and its more modern historical developments, to make Ireland's history a continuum of themes and events repeating themselves over the years, and to mark the anguish in the decisions of her great leaders.

Because there is much of the tale teller, the antiquarian, the poet and the balladeer in Colum, and because these are the chief ingredients in this last cycle of plays, they are better than any he has written since his early days in the Irish theatre.

They were followed in 1967 by the dramatic adaptation and performance of his poetry under the titles *The Road Round Ireland* and, later in its off-Broadway production, *Carricknabauna*. The dramatization was staged in Norwalk, Connecticut by Basil Burwell and was favorably received. In its New York production the poetry was interspersed with extraneous stage business and pointless, banal movement which was designed to make it palatable to a New York audience. As a result the poetry was lost in the mire of gimmickry, and the play failed.

As I have suggested in the preceding pages, any overall assessment of Colum as a dramatist would be less than candid if it did not admit that his chief contributions to the stage were historical rather than literary. While his importance to the Irish theatre cannot be overstated, his contributions were noteworthy because they were precedents rather than because they were destined some day to be recognized masterpieces of drama. Many of Colum's plays had merit, but none, in the final analysis, could be called great, as can a number of his poems. On the other hand, it has already been shown that his poetry has depended in large measure on his dramatic background and techniques, and to the extent that his poetry enters into his last plays it has improved them. It is difficult to imagine Colum not writing for the theatre. Without the influence and experience of his playwriting, we would have had a poet and storyteller of a vastly different and less important kind.

4

Fiction, Biographies, Essays

Most students of Irish literature know Padraic Colum as a poet, a dramatist and perhaps even a writer of children's stories. It may come as a surprise that he has written a considerable number of short stories, two novels, two biographies and four books of essays, as well as contributions and prefaces for fifty-one books and pieces of various sorts for more than sixty newspapers and periodicals. The scope of this study does not permit a survey of them all, but some attempt will be made to include Colum's major books and to give a more detailed analysis of his most ambitious and, I believe, best prose work, *The Flying Swans*.

Despite the diverse nature of the work I am here considering, when Colum's fiction and nonfiction prose are considered as a whole, certain patterns begin to manifest themselves; altogether these patterns comprise a style distinctive as that of any writer of the twentieth century. My remarks in this chapter will not include Colum's children's stories because their number and relative importance dictate a separate section.

Almost all of Colum's fiction grows out of its Irish milieu, and similarly most of his nonfiction is an elaboration on the country, its people and its customs. There have been excursions to Hawaii, France and America but the bulk of his work concerns his home. Because of this preoccupation he has become for many Americans the window on the Irish scene, the chronicler of its folklore and customs, a sort of literary tourist bureau. Though this role had its inception in his early poetry and plays, he has striven to maintain it through his novels, biographies and essays.

Just as his subject matter is predominantly Irish, his style can also be generally described as familiar and colloquial. His most characteristic stylistic trait is his abundant use of the present tense narration in fiction as well as nonfiction. This together with a first person narrator places him in the role of a storyteller sitting by a turf fire spinning out tales of things familiar to him and wondrous to his audience. This posture that Colum tries to maintain in his work is one he is well suited to. The particular criteria of excellence in evaluating Colum's work are not the normal currency of contemporary literary critics, because few other serious writers attempt what he is doing, and our appreciation of it has fallen into disrepair through disuse. Part of my intention in the survey which follows is to place his prose works in better perspective.

Padraic Colum has been publishing short stories consistently over a period of sixty years from the early days of *The United Irishman* to his more recent contributions to *The New Yorker*. Two short books of stories, *Studies* (Dublin 1907) and *Three Men* (London 1930), demonstrate the range of Colum's fiction from romanticism through realism to light-hearted satire. *Studies* contains the narrative "The Miracle of the Corn" (See Chapter 2) and two short stories, "Eilis: A Woman's Story" and "The Flute Player's Story."

The first of these reflects the dark mysteries of a nineteenth-century romance, the second the thoroughly realistic attitude which was to permeate his writing in *Thomas Muskerry* and after. The first story, like Joyce's "Eveline," deals with a girl who cannot bring herself to cross the last ditch which separates her from her lover. It carries strong overtones of *The Fiddler's House*, and later, when Eilis marries a middle class, unromantic husband instead of the lover she would not go to, it is reminiscent of Joyce's "The Dead." The similarity to "The Dead" is heightened by the name of Eilis's husband, Michael Conroy, a combination of Joyce's Michael Furey and Gabriel Conroy. "Eilis" reflects the influence Joyce was to have on his friend's fiction. In this story Colum develops the narrative technique which he characteristically employs in many later works: that is, he begins in the first person and then introduces an internal narrator whose voice we actually hear for the duration of the tale. Seldom, however, are the narrators anything other than reporters.

In "The Flute Player's Story" the stark realities of the marital state are manifest in a vignette of a woman who marries for love rather than for prudence and lives to regret it. Again the sifting of the narration through two narrators removes us three times from the tale and makes us see it as some sort of an allegory even in its realism. Colum refuses to intrude a moral, since the flute player-narrator Mrs. Sarsfield might have married is even more disgusting in his own way than the man she did marry. In this grim tale Colum balances the metaphysics of "The Miracle of the Corn" and the romance of "Eilis" with a new kind of realism which was only then coming to have literary consequence.

Three Men, at the other end of the spectrum in time and in intent, is almost unique in Colum's writing. A longish narrative about the pretensions of the Eblana Literary Society, it is the only extended piece of satire that Colum ever attempted. This genuinely funny story proves what must have occurred to anyone who has read much of Colum's work: that he is an exceptionally able comic writer when he chooses to be. All through his prose there runs an undercurrent of humor, a view of the ludicrousness of life. It runs like an underground stream bubbling up here and there but seldom surfacing for the entire duration of a story or essay. This humor is especially remarkable when we consider that at the turn of the century there was a real reluctance among Irish writers who took themselves seriously to portray any character who might be labeled a "stage Irishman," and I do not think Colum ever completely rid himself of this hesitation.

Nevertheless *Three Men* is an exquisitely Irish satire about the pomposity of would-be intellectuals. The group consists of Howard Todd-Grubb, a street photographer; Anthony Tisdil, whose newly achieved social status in the world and invitation to the society meeting are due to the fact that he was in a railway accident the day before; Charles Hempson, a drunken newspaper editor; Mr. Greally, who looks like St. Michael; and Loftus Mongan, whose health has been impaired with cheap food and whose paper "The Illuminati," will be the main event in the Eblana Literary Society program.

The meeting proceeds through a number of mishaps including no less than two seemingly interminable readings of Mongan's paper and a scuffle when the drunken editor is thrown out. There is a reassertion of the manhood of Anthony Tisdil as he shatters his Walter Mitty mould of timidity to eject Hempson from the room. The climax of the story comes with the second reading of Mongan's paper and its effect on Tisdil.

> As for Anthony Tisdil he was caught up and held by a title that Loftus Mongan introduced early into his address and frequently made use of—"The Illuminati." All that was to be achieved was to be achieved through the Illuminati. And the Illuminati were those present who were sharing in the thoughts that were being delivered by Loftus Mongan.[1]

Like most satire, *Three Men* is topical. It no doubt reflects something of Colum's sentiment regarding pseudo-intellectuals and it probably has particular reference to some aspects of the Irish literary movement. For example it should be noted that the Eblana Debating Society was the name given to a group organized by Arthur Griffith. It is a shame that Colum did not write more comedy, for *Three Men* was indeed a promising beginning.

Colum's greatest achievement as a fiction writer was not to come until much later in his life with the publication of the second of his two novels, *The Flying Swans*. Because the first, which enjoyed far more critical acclaim when it was printed, afforded a necessary preparation for the second, it should be given some consideration here.

Castle Conquer has all of the flaws one would expect from a writer who had never before attempted a long piece of fiction. It is a romance set in the late 1870's and early 80's having as its background the struggle against the oppressive landholders who preceded the uprisings of the early twentieth century. The young protagonists, Brighid Moynagh and Francis Gillick, must undergo the torments of their own youthful temperaments and community censure as well as the persecution of a tyrannical system. Throughout the first half of the book one feels that the young lovers, especially Francis, are getting themselves into trouble with willful acts of irresponsibility, but as the consequences of their passionate and reckless love become clear, the reader feels more and more the encroachments of Irish nationalistic propaganda altering the motivations of the couple and the artistic integrity of the book.

Although Colum's accurate ear for Irish speech is as apparent in *Castle Conquer* as it is in *The Flying Swans*, I will defer a fuller discussion of this aspect of style until the discussion of the latter novel. Colum also includes such typically Irish literary devices as the indispensable informer, the occult mysticism of the road people, and a plethora of dreams and omens.

Further, *Castle Conquer* affords the first example of what was to become a favorite format of the author in such later works as *The Flying Swans* and the Noh plays: the relationship of recurring action to a place. The plot of *Castle Conquer* centers around the castle itself and around O'Failey's tower, which Gillick's ancestor built and which is the site of the protagonist's commitment to the Irish militant movement. At the end of the book Francis returns to the castle in triumph with the Irish Republican Army to hear the proclamation of an Irish freestate. Gillick is reminiscent of the heroic chieftains of the Irish sagas as he fights his way through what seem to be overwhelming odds and in victory is finally able to hand the struggle on to future generations of children and grandchildren.

In order to suggest a long continuum of time, a requisite of the heroic saga Colum envisioned, he added an epilogue to the novel which updates the action by forty years. The book ends quite satisfactorily before this with Gillick's serving a three-year prison term for his conspiracy against the landowners, and the reader accepts the hero's punishment as the last of the trials he and his paramour, Brighid Moynagh, must face. He has been impetuous, she impulsive. His motive of patriotism, and hers of passion, have led them into indiscretions for which they have now made retribution through the public exposure of their love affair and his jail sentence. This is really a satisfactory conclusion to the novel, but Colum tries to give the book unwarranted scope by appending the epilogue. Thus Gillick, who has really done little more than beat a few bailiffs with a hurly stick and make ambitious plans, is forced into the role of an epic hero of the stature of Brian Boru. In order to make this aggrandizement credible, the author recites in the epilogue a list of deeds which Gillick has performed between his release from prison and the concluding capitulation of the British. But since the reader has not witnessed these deeds, he cannot accept them as an integral part of the action of the novel. Hence, the end, with its implications of heroism, seems inflated.

Other mistakes mar the effectiveness of the book. The inclusion of such fairly lengthy tangents as the story of the origin of "the long dance" are interesting in themselves but have no organic function in the action. But the most obvious of the novel's shortcomings is its propagandistic tendencies. These often lack subtlety and act upon the reader like a moral bludgeon. For instance, the description of Eglish leaves the reader with little to judge for himself.

> In that town all the streets led to the goal: it was on a hill and it had a considerable area. In that town there were

three public buildings—the courthouse, the workhouse and the gaol, and the three had been built at a time when labour was cheap, and stone, apparently, plentiful; out of these three buildings the town, if it were shattered, might be built up again, as a town might be built out of a quarry that was a Roman ruin. These three buildings registered the will of a racial ascendency—the will to dominate harshly.[2]

Francis Gillick was obviously intended to be one of Ireland's deliverers from these evils, and if Colum has not succeeded in casting him as an epic hero, the author has not left him wholly without credentials for his role as emancipator. He is a member of the ancient Irish aristocracy. Family ties and bloodlines hence become a major motif of the book. This theme, which is to recur as a main motif of *The Flying Swans,* is to its heritage minded author part of the heroic idea.

The other major aspect of Colum's concept of heredity is that of the natural dignity and nobility of the common Irish people. This motif is implicit in all of Colum's work, but nowhere is it spelled out as explicitly as in *Castle Conquer.*

The moment that Sir John Seagrave's agent was to be brought into the house the peasants became at once nobles: they listened to him with dignity; they treated him with consideration, and it was all done as if a whole stately tradition was embodied in the brother and sister and the two young girls.[3]

The political aspects of the novel are based upon another theme central to the Colum canon, one which we have seen before in his plays: the love for the land. *Castle Conquer* represents the tyranny of the land usurping establishment, and Francis Gillick's enmity is aroused by the plight of a peasant, Martin Jordan, who is about to be evicted. But the allegory of land ownership does not end there. It can become an unwholesome force as well as a positive one. Honor Paralon, Brighid's foster mother, has a lust for the land which rivals the tyrannical landowner's. She plots and bargains to acquire the very land which Francis Gillick has been fighting to save for Jordan.

Castle Conquer is thus by no means an uninteresting book. The love story is poignant, the action for the most part absorbing and realistic, and the characters believable. Despite its flaws the book did produce a number of themes and characters which Colum was later able to employ in such widely diversified works as *The Flying Swans* and *Poet's Circuits*. For example the theme of the drives and obligations of aristocracy comes to full fruition in *The Flying Swans* which has as its protagonist "Ulick O'Rehill . . . a Milesian [Celtic, Irish-Catholic aristocrat] and the son of a Milesian, as his genealogically minded paternal relatives would say." [4] Also, Owen Paralon, Brighid's uncle, a character patterned after Colum's own granduncle, reappears to provide part of the narrative line of *Poet's Circuits*. *Castle Conquer* is therefore a fair attempt at a first novel, an attempt which, while it had its flaws, was not completely lacking in value in its own right, as well as providing a model for the first rate novel which was to follow.

Colum's second novel, *The Flying Swans*, was ten years in preparation before it was finally published by Crown in 1957. Parts of it were printed in the *Dial* while the text was still in progress. Van Wyck Brooks, who calls the book "A moving and beautiful evocation of an Irish boyhood in a timeless world of country sights and sounds," [5] seems to have been the only major critic to have had anything to say about the novel. *The Flying Swans* received a mildly deprecatory review in the New York *Times* [6] but otherwise has passed unnoticed. When it was translated into German, however, its reception in Germany was a great deal more favorable and enthusiastic. Colum had originally intended the novel to be the first of a trilogy on the artist, the soldier, and the priest. The plan was abandoned, however, when Padraic became discouraged about the lack of enthusiasm over *The Flying Swans*. The apathy with which the book was greeted stemmed, I think, from the fact that by the time it appeared the critics had already categorized Colum's work as consisting of dated Irish plays, good folk poetry and innocuous children's stories. A story about a youngster's life in Ireland would seem to fit the preconceived pattern. This one does not.

The Flying Swans is the best single prose work that Colum has written. It is as good as most of his poetry and far surpasses his drama. Because the book has not received the attention it deserved it will be treated here as extensively as this study permits.

The novel is well constructed, written in a language which is always striking and often beautiful, and searching in its themes. It is a *Bildungsroman* influenced by those Irish sagas dealing with expulsion and return of the Irish heroes and by *The Mabinogion,* the series of Welsh romances concerning the youthful exploits of various Celtic heroes. The novel traces its protagonist, Ulick O'Rehill, from his birth to young adulthood.

Though Colum was writing fairy stories as his main source of income during the more than ten years that *The Flying Swans* was in progress, there is little of the childlike fantasy which was to make his children's books so popular. The world he describes in his book is realistic, if undatable. His Irish countryside is populated with lifelike characters who are unique even if their identities as types of Irish peasantry seem familiar.

One of the most remarkable things about Colum's fiction as well as his drama and poetry is his ability to reproduce so accurately the nuances of Irish speech, particularly the midland dialect. *The Flying Swans* is no exception to this rule. In both narration and dialogue the novel abounds in such Irish expressions as *bychild* for *bastard, behindhand* for *behind,* and *fornenst* for *in front of.* Other more usual Irish expressions like *myself, himself* and *herself* as direct objects also appear in the narration and dialogue, but these are not uncommon in Irish letters.

If many writers use the Irish idiom, none do it so completely as Colum and few so well. He conveys the

Irish lilt not only in his choice of words, but also in his ordering of them. For example he very often reverses past participle and verb ("when he had a sup taken") [7] and subject and predicate adjective ("Oh, very poor was the boy's mother").[8] This produces the downward cadence and tone of voice at the end of the phrase or sentence which is characteristic of Irish speech. Colum also enriches the rhythms of his prose by occasionally repeating words, especially polysyllabic words, for no apparent reason beyond the sensuous quality of the sound ("On this day pigs were grunting and grunting in its street").[9] Often these word repetitions give the narrative a fairy-tale aspect as in the following example:

> Over the abandoned premises which had been a harness maker's establishment was a horse's head. But to mention it merely as a horse's head is to understate the significance it had for Ulick O'Rehill. It managed to be a very significant horse's head.[10]

Because the inverted syntax, the cadenced speech and the word and phrase repetition are all indigenous to poetry, it is not surprising to find that a good deal of *The Flying Swans* sounds much like a poem. Colum's prosodic style helps capture in his peasant characters the natural dignity their counterparts possess in life.

Colum lends to the formality of his narrative by frequently giving formal introductions to various narrative segments and stories the characters relate.

> "Tell me about her," he said. She was ready enough to inform him; this was the substance of what the old woman gabbed: . . ."[11]

The device is one used extensively in Colum's children's stories to make them appear more magnificent and meaningful in the eyes of their audience. While American readers may at first find this particularly Irish use of words and word order a bit disconcerting, the devices wear well and are easy to accept after a few chapters of *The Flying Swans*.

Though the narrative perspective of the novel is third

person, it parallels fairly closely the impressions and feelings of the protagonist. The events that make the greatest impression on the youngster, like the death and funeral of his grandfather, Breasal O'Breasal, are given predominance. Colum followed the pattern Joyce set in *A Portrait of the Artist* by constructing a novel of impressions as well as events.

Occasionally, like Joyce, Colum briefly shifts his narrative perspective to enhance the impressions of one of the minor characters. For instance, in a description of the stable boy's regard for the political activities of Robert O'Rehill, Ulick's father, Colum gives the following third person account:

> It was a sight to see O'Rehill on the platform with the *bolom skiahs* around him—friezecoats that hadn't enough land to sod a lark and blackcoats fornenst them that prated so much that the town was sick and tired of them. And then an oul' fellow in the crowd, one of those grey-coated lads, who think they are as famed for their discourse as Dan O'Connell, shouted up to him, "What would their reverends say to that, your Honour?" Oh, very dry he was! [12]

The narrative line is reminiscent of the barfly's in the Cyclops chapter of Joyce's *Ulysses*. Colum is especially fond of the Cyclops narrator and may indeed have had this narrative technique in mind when he wrote the passage.

Colum uses his Irish-English to evoke some excellent descriptive passages. His pig-slaughtering scene is horribly real in its approximation of the callousness of mankind and its effect on Ulick's brother, Breasal, the little boy in a hostile place who is made to participate in it. The crowd gathered around the yard sound as if they were in the Colosseum as they yell for blood, while the last of the magnificently disdainful gladiators, a big sow, comes to the center of the arena.

> Out of a sty a large sow marched as if she wanted to know what all the ruction was about. He was glad she was not yoked for the slaughter, for there was something about

her, her independence maybe, that appealed to the one who was here on sufferance. The yard was hers, it seemed, no matter how many of her kind were struck there. She stood in the middle of the yard and made water. But one and another swing of the hammer came on her; she screamed in a grieved, surprised way, and was left lying in the middle of the yard. Breasal felt as if he had seen an execution.[13]

When Ulick's mother has a stillborn child he must go to the cemetery with the body in a shoe box and bury it. Ulick's meeting with his father in the graveyard and their talk over the shallow grave comprise a poignant scene in which the uncompromising reality of the description belies any notion that Colum is capable of writing only sentimental, folksy Irish pieces.

Colum uses a number of symbols in *The Flying Swans,* some apparent, others more obscure. The most prominent is of course the swans themselves. The birds appear at the major junctures of the protagonist's career. The first reference to the swans is interwoven in a complex symbol pattern occurring at the time of the birth of Breasal.

Then suddenly he heard a creaking noise; it was over his head: when he looked up he thought a goose had taken to its wings and was flying towards the river. Then he knew that the wide-winged bird was a swan. His spirit lifted, knowing he was watching a seldom-seen flight, the proud, strong-winged bird making for some new habitation. Oh, but it was grand to watch that flight! He went in its direction and, crossing the river at the shallows, came to where he had often wanted to go, to the place that had the tower and the ancient crosses. . . . He saw that the back and front and sides of the crosses had raised figures of men and animals around them, and around the circles were lacings and knots. There was something wonderful in the minds of the men who carved a stone into this and, as with a hundred stories, crowded it with such curious figures.[14]

Breasal eventually will provide the means to Ulick's freedom from the tyranny of his burden of heredity, as we shall subsequently see. The swans mark a turning point in Ulick's life here. In order to grasp the significance of the scene and the swans which introduce it, we must be cognizant of another symbol pattern which appears here, the cemetery to which the swans have led him and what it represents. In this initial scene of Breasal's birth and the swans' flight, Ulick first perceives the cemetery, where the wonder of the monument makers' creation is the beginning of his eventual salvation. He will one day, like the craftsmen who carve the crosses and figures he so admires, seek a living as a stonecutter to provide both his way in his mortal life and his share of immortality through his artistic works.

If cemeteries are paradoxically a means of hope, they also provide the source of the youngster's trial and despair.

> Ah, but the men who built the tower and made the crosses and carved the figures—he would never know them; they had gone forever. And for himself, what was there but what was going on in the house where his mother moaned and a child was being born from her as a calf from the cow.[15]

Robert O'Rehill's great failing is his inability to extricate himself from the tyranny of his own paternity and the Irish nobility which he tries vainly to emulate. His all-consuming ambitions and the family's ruination are entombed in the cemetery, and the juxtaposition of the relative claims of life and death which become apparent to the boy at this moment of insight have never been fully understood nor their priorities apparent to his father.

As Ulick stands in the cemetery reflecting on his loneliness, the birds ascend again, this time heralding the news of the birth of someone to end his solitude.

> How lonesome it was! How lonesome!
> Above his head there was a sound. It was the creaking of wings. He saw flying swans—more than one. Something that was strong like their wings and free like their flight

came to him. Then, hearing somebody shouting, he went back to the pasture.

Here was his grandfather coming towards him. When Breasal O'Breasal neared he said, "Your mother wants you —go back now." "Is my mother safe?" "She is, and you have a little brother." [16]

The sought-after freedom which is betokened by the swans will come to Ulick through his responsibility for and the companionship of his brother.

The swans appear again when Ulick's mother, forced to live by her own devices after she and her children have been abandoned by her husband, arranges to take over a shop in Cairnthual after Breasal's birth. As the family prepares for departure the swans again are flying overhead, this time conveying the realization of freedom from her family, the O'Breasals, with whom she has been forced to live while her child was being born, and the advent of opportunity, which the new arrangements will offer the O'Rehills.

The next appearance of the birds occurs after the death of Ulick's mother when the O'Rehills are again forced to take refuge with her family. Again they presage a momentous event in the book, coming just prior to Ulick's seeing but not recognizing his father after a number of years. The love which Ulick had held for his father is now nearly exhausted by Robert's denial of Breasal's paternity, but Ulick still must confront his father to make peace. As the swans take off Ulick sees a hooded man whom he later discovers to be his father, and the stage is set for the long awaited confrontation essential to the attainment of Ulick's maturity.

The last appearance of the swans, at the end of the book, is a confirmation of Ulick's final emancipation. Now the brothers no longer need their father's affirmation.

"Yes, Breasal," he said, "you will see our father one of these days. And it won't be that you'll want him to say that he is your father, but that he'll want you to say that you are his son." [17]

The swans, appearing at major events in Ulick's life, have thus signified his growth through the trials of an exceptionally difficult youth into adulthood, with its attendant freedom and responsibility.

Another major symbol of *The Flying Swans* is a sculptured horse's head. Like many of Joyce's symbols in *A Portrait of the Artist*, this head derives its meaning from the importance the protagonist attaches to it: "The curious thing about it was that, as it became more familiar, it became more significant to the boy who passed it day after day." [18] The head hangs over what was formerly a harness-maker's shop bearing the name "Bonfils." "And after he had heard her name, without knowing or caring whether it was correct or not, he connected this name with the one the yellow-haired girl had—Christine Bondfield." [19] His suspicions later prove correct for she is from the same family. The horse is a symbol of Ulick's adolescence and his initiation into manhood, and it is Christine who is finally high priestess at the rites. The horse acts, like the swans, as a multiple symbol linking various elements of the story and foreshadowing coming events. The fact that it is linked with a harness-maker prefigures the return of Ulick's errant father who pursues the trade of harness-making. Just as Ulick feels his destiny is inextricably bound to the horse's head, so it comes to represent a symbol of his father. The name "Bonfils," or good son, tends to underscore the father-son implications the head holds for the boy. In times of difficulty, such as his father's involvement with a local prostitute, the sensual aspects of the horse image become enlarged in Ulick's mind.

> He even gave up looking at that lonely, consoling image, the horse's head over the harness maker's shop; if he stopped before it some boy would come along and try to sound him about his father and Nannie Toland, enlarging it in gross, vulgar, degrading descriptiveness.[20]

But the image evolves finally into a wholesome symbol through another of Ulick's flirtations.

Veronica Grace calls the horse Shanglan after the horse of the ancient mythical hero, Cuchulainn,[21] and as the platonic but romantic affair between herself and Ulick progresses, the horse is closely linked to her regard for him. Ulick adopts this view of himself for a while and his perspective of the horse changes with it.

> Across the street old Shanglan's head had brightness on it; the rain had splashed it, taking off stains; the sun shone on it, making it, for all its acknowledged loneliness, brave. Young O'Rehill was made glad by the look of career it showed. It had looked on all the days of his schoolgoing and now it looked on his school-leaving.[22]

In a way the Nugent girl helps to create self-confidence in Ulick as her granduncle, Baron Nugent, did with Robert. The difference is that Robert's assurance was self-destructive, leading him to a world in which he could not hope to compete, while Ulick's permits him to pull together successfully the shreds of the family and assume a meaningful position in life.

There are several other more traditional symbols to which Ulick gives meaning: the great blossoming laburnum tree in the Comyns' yard, which Ulick takes for a symbol of his new life; Thomas Moore's "Fire Worshippers" poem, a symbol of the passions of Ulick's youth; a wild carnival ride with Christine reminiscent of D. H. Lawrence's "Tickets, Please" and its aftermath of letdown, suggesting post-orgastic catharsis and a foreshadowing of the end of the affair between the two young lovers; and "The Henwife's Son," a rags to riches story which Ulick demands to hear as a child and which underlies the dilemma of his father's desperate bid for fame and fortune, a sense of misplaced values which Ulick must purge in himself.

Colum divided his novel into ten sections, each consisting of from seven to seventeen chapters. The smaller divisions deal with specific scenes and events while the larger correspond to various stages of Ulick's and Breasal's life and maturity. The novel begins in the market town of Dooard and follows the travels and fortunes of the family of Robert O'Rehill throughout Ireland until it comes full cycle back to Dooard and history begins again. The cyclical aspect of the book can be largely attributed, as can a number of other scenes and devices, to Joyce, to whom, along with James Stephens, the novel is dedicated.

Echoes of Joyce are audible also in the relationship of the brothers, reminiscent of *Stephen Hero*, and the vicarious father-son relation of Duineen and Ulick, closely resembling that of Bloom and Stephen in *Ulysses*.[23] There is even the ritual cocoa to complete the consummation of the relationship in *The Flying Swans*.

> Ulick was in two minds about what he should do—perhaps show Duineen the O'Rehills were not to be patronized by declining the proffered cocoa and then walking out without taking the book. He ended by drinking his cocoa silently and then taking the book as if it were a sort of burthen. He gave Duineen a mere good night as he went off the premises.[24]

Like the Stephen of *A Portrait of the Artist* and *Ulysses*, Ulick is an exceptionally solitary character, but like the protagonist of *Stephen Hero*, he has a brother who will be his link with the rest of the world, and who will in *The Flying Swans* be the source of his salvation.

Not only is the setting cyclical but also the principal dilemma of the book: the O'Rehills' search for identity. The generation preceding Robert O'Rehill had but one goal: to restore to the family the confiscated land, the noble line and the family identity. Robert, torn between his passion and his duty to reëstablish the grandeur of his ancestry, founders upon the shoals of his inability to determine his place in life, and so gives up what he has gained for a vain attempt to become a national figure in politics. Then in frustration he reverts to the passion of his youth and abandons his family and country, fails at even his love affair, and returns to Ireland twice more in other fruitless attempts at establishing some sort of identity for himself, his last effort taking the form of a wild identification with the pagan version of St. Augustine. He manages to pass his dilemma on to his children, Ulick, who must decide either to lead a responsible life or a passionate one, and Breasal, whose paternity is challenged, and who must find out literally who he is before he can even begin to assume the struggle toward a responsible life. Each generation is plagued by the mistakes of the preceding. Ulick's solution is much like the one offered in *The Catcher in the Rye*: He finds his own salvation in his responsibility for his brother, and an acceptance of the hand life has dealt him.

The cyclical pattern prevails all through the father-son dilemma of the book as various events in the father's life repeat themselves in the son's.[25] The horse on Bonfils' harness shop is one example of this. Two girls, Christine Bondfield and Veronica Grace, are associated with the horse. Christine is linked with passion as was Margery Plunkett, Robert's paramour, and Veronica with social advancement, as was Monica Owens, the girl Robert's father had picked out as the prospective mistress of The Abbey, the family homestead. With Christine, Ulick relives his father's passion, while an advantageous liaison with Veronica becomes, as was the case a generation before, nothing more than a possibility. While Christine's love for Ulick is passionate, like her predecessor, Margery, she chooses security with Twambley rather than the dictates of her heart.

When the young people play follow-the-leader, Ulick tries to assert his manhood and identity before Claire Comyn, but he can only emulate his father's mistakes by leading the party onto other people's property, being caught trespassing and ignominiously falling into a quarry, breaking his leg. Finally, he, like his father, considers running away only to be held back by the chance circumstance of a mix-up in messages. The difference in the two generations lies in the father's complete refusal to acknowledge his responsibility for the paternity of his second son, while Ulick attains manhood by accepting the responsibility for his brother.

This responsibility means that Ulick must compel his father to admit that Breasal is his son in order to free Breasal from the bondage of uncertain identity which O'Rehill has cast over him. The physical conflict that Ulick must engage in is not finally with his father but with Lem Grabbitt, a tinker who has virtually held Breasal captive and who stands *in loco parentis* to Breasal. Grabbitt, the only wholly evil character in the book, is in a number of ways like Robert O'Rehill. The tinker's transient life parallels that of his counterpart, while his occupation of repairing pots is much like O'Rehill's harness repair trade. He has forced his wife to destroy a new baby just as O'Rehill has virtually brought about the death of his stillborn child, and now he holds Breasal captive just as Robert does with his denial that he is Breasal's father.

Ulick does a form of battle with both men, on one hand getting Robert to admit that he had lied, and on the other physically coming to grips with Grabbitt. The battle between Ulick and Grabbitt is much like the one between Paul Morel and Baxter Dawes in *Sons and Lovers*. In order to purge the rivalry existing between Paul and his father, in that case over an Oedipal fixation in which Clara Dawes supplants Paul's mother, Paul finally fights with Dawes and later is able to become friendly with him and bring about his own eventual freedom from the awful burden of his own fixation. In *The Flying Swans* the dilemma is not Oedipal, but one of bondage to the cycle of misconceptions about the ultimate values of life handed down from generation to generation. By coming to grips with this bondage both through the vicarious battle with Grabbitt and through the confrontation with Robert, Ulick wins freedom for himself and his brother from the old tyrannies of reëstablishing the O'Rehill name, freedom to live their own lives as best they can. These two confrontation scenes provide the climax of the book and its philosophical basis.

Colum has treated the theme of vain, inordinate am-

bition before in *The Land, Balloon,* and *Thomas Muskerry,* but never has he given it such a complete solution. At the conclusion of the novel the boys are free
from their father and free to pursue the trades of common people, rather than chase genealogical phantoms.
The last note is one of hope, an affirmation of Colum's
basic optimism.

Though *The Flying Swans,* like the bulk of Colum's
work, is striking on first reading, principally for its cadenced Irish language and its realistic images and description, this novel also has the depth and durability of
structure, theme and characterization that withstand
and reward repeated reading. It is a book which deserves
far more critical attention that it has received.

We next consider perhaps Colum's least-known role,
that of biographer. He undertook each of his two biographies because he wanted to set the record straight about
people whom he knew intimately. *Our Friend James
Joyce* was a labor purely of love while *Ourselves Alone*
was a matter of duty mixed with devotion. Each of these
books is interesting, though the Joyce book is a far more
stylized, personal account than the Griffith volume.

To begin with, the Griffith biography is not wholly
about Arthur Griffith. Though the Irish edition is entitled *Arthur Griffith* (1872–1922), the full title of the
American edition, *Ourselves Alone: The Story of Arthur
Griffith and the Origin of the Irish Free State,* gives a
more accurate idea of what the book was all about. It
deals far less with the details of Griffith's life than it does
with the events surrounding the birth of the *Sinn Fein*
party and the free state. Unlike anything else Colum has
written, this historical account is very heavily documented and scholarly in tone, with relatively few of the
personal reminiscences that characterize his other work.

Colum began his book at the behest of the friends and
leaders of Arthur Griffith's pro-treaty party, to "set
things right," so it is inevitable that the account should
be slanted in the direction of the pro-treaty faction and
against the *Fianna Fáil* party now in power in Ireland.

This impeded the publication and reviews of the book in Ireland, for the animosities of the civil war were still felt in Irish politics. The biography has, however, enjoyed brisk sales in Ireland as well as in the United States.

That this account of Griffith's period, one of the most fascinating in Irish history, makes absorbing reading is due in part to its inherent interest and in part to Colum's style. He begins the book, like the epic he means it to be, *in medias res*, with Griffith signing the long-awaited treaty with England. The narrative then returns to trace the history of the event to its origins before proceeding to the battle over the document and Griffith's death and aftermath in Ireland. Though the biography is essentially a scholarly piece of research, it does contain editorial passages and even now and then a Macaulayesque dramatic flourish.

> Combativeness and again combativeness! That was the idea that Parnell embodied. Where was this combativeness to be used? Anywhere, everywhere, but immediately at the salient of British authority, the House of Commons.[26]

A great deal of the literary value as well as historical importance of the book comes from the personal knowledge and intimacy that Colum had with Griffith and the events of those fateful years at the turn of the century. For example a fictional, romantic account of the arrival of arms for the insurgents at Howth could not have been much more glamorous and at the same time more life-like than Colum's.

> The present writer was fortunate enough to have been present at the landing of the rifles on that forenoon in July 1914. As they were handed up, the packing straw stripped off them, as each along the quayside handled and passed the rifle down the chain of Volunteers, a thrill went through each man of them. A barrier had been broken down. A part of the conquest had been undone.[27]

Unfortunately for the devotees of Colum's impressionistic style, there is all too little of this sort of personal revelation in the work. Colum tells us in the introduction that after he had rejected the original offer to write the book, Sean Milroy had consented and had amassed a considerable amount of scholarship in a first draft before he died. When Colum finally consented to write the biography, he was given the great body of original documents and research which Milroy had compiled, and, no doubt, felt himself obliged to use it. There are, however, some impressions which are more like those of the poet than the historian. For example, Colum describes Edward Carson as follows:

> The present writer saw him only once, and then for less than five minutes. Appearing on a platform, he spoke to some leading personages with the aloofness of one who had greater affairs on his mind than were there engaging them. His eyes were remarkably hollow and his mouth was remarkably tightened. Garbed in black, his height was commanding. Abruptly he left. There must have been something in him that approved of what he was doing, but his whole demeanour was that of a joyless man going on joyless errands.[28]

Occasionally Colum goes too far in expressing opinions and one feels personal conviction overriding objectivity and historical evidence, as in the case of Erskine Childers, a man whom Griffith, and later his biographer, disliked intensely for little apparent reason other than his English ties and his stand on the treaty with England. For the most part, however, Colum writes carefully and uses a fairly consistent mixture of fact and stylistic flair, a combination which has traditionally differentiated great biographies from dull recitals of fact. He is ever conscious of the fact that he is writing for an American as well as an Irish audience, and explains things like The Dublin Castle and what it stood for, which is commonplace knowledge in Ireland but may be unfamiliar to Americans.

Our Friend James Joyce, Colum's second biography, was written in collaboration with his wife, Mary. She planned the shape of the narrative and wrote about a third of the actual text. She was working on the book when she died, and Colum, who had discussed it extensively with her, finished the task she had laid out. Joyce's early life in Dublin is left to Colum, while Mary concentrates on their later friendship in Paris. Her sections tend to be more literal and to dwell on the factual side of their relations with the Joyces, while Colum's sections are more whimsical and concentrate more on Joyce's literature than does the principally biographical detail Mary gives.

Because most of the book is Padraic's and because he has chosen an impressionistic approach for his sections, *Our Friend James Joyce* is vastly different from *Ourselves Alone*. Colum's loose and fanciful narrative style, seen only briefly in *Ourselves Alone*, is the predominant characteristic of the Joyce biography. Colum outlines his narrative principle early in the book.

> I should say here that the chronology of our sojourns in Paris during the late 1920's and early 1930's is something of a tangled skein. It is probable that encounters my wife and I had with the Joyces that were later than others will be written of as prior, and the other way around. I am depending, in my part, upon my memory, which is a lively one. And where character, incident, and speech are the important things, chronology does not so much matter.[29]

What a contrast to the painstaking, heavily researched and documented history of *Ourselves Alone*! It is clear that Colum was not trying as in the Griffith biography to give a complete, factually accurate history of a long, complicated period in Irish history, but rather trying to capture the essence of a man he knew well and to relate what he knew about this man to Joyce's works. For this reason there is a great deal of allusion to various Joyce works, most noticeably his poetry and *Finnegans Wake*.

Through personal anecdotes Colum concentrates on dispelling what he considered the mythology of Joyce. For instance Colum describes a scene which indicates the affection which existed between Joyce and his father, despite the impression Joyce may have conveyed in *A Portrait of the Artist.*

> A spacious saloon called The Yellow House, some way out into the country, was their terminus. In a big room, empty at the time, there were two pianos. Refreshment having been ordered, the older man sat at one. He played a theme that asked, "Why did you go from us?" His son "Jim," at the other piano, played something in reply (he told me what it was, but I cannot remember). It was an epiphany of a sort, a showing forth of a relationship which was nearly always covered over, and Joyce dwelt on it later with some tenderness.[30]

Colum also quite unsystematically sheds what light he can on several of Joyce's works. I think his concentration on the poetry and *Finnegans Wake* was not so much due to his lack of knowledge about Joyce's works as the fact that Colum's closest associations with Joyce in Dublin and Paris coincided with the writing of these things. Colum quotes freely from the poetry in setting Joyce's mood and illuminates certain obscure and personal references in the *Wake.* His heaviest critical concentration is on that book, and he even goes so far as to reproduce practically all of his own introduction to a major sequence, *Anna Livia Plurabelle,* as it was published by Crosby Gaige in New York in 1928.

But the chief virtue of the biography, for all its illumination of obscure Joycean references, is to catch the spirit of the Colums' genius friend. That it does so in such an interesting fashion is due, like the success of their marriage, to the complementary styles and personalities of the Colums: Mary, factual, analytical, demanding; Padraic, fanciful, introspective, philosophical; but both possessing a lively humor and a sense of the ludicrous. Padraic's account of his visit to the French opera, at Joyce's behest, to hear the singer, John Sullivan, captures some of this:

> Surrounded by busts of singers and composers, and by functionaries wearing chains that made them look like

chancellors of universities and by others who had the appearance of high military and civic officials, I was made to realize that the prestige of the French opera, bound up, seemingly, with that of the French state, was not to be infringed upon.[31]

Colum is able to augment his humor with a poet's knack for a representative image or fact which will capture and summarize a feeling or mood, such as the ribald, satiric relationship between Joyce and Gogarty during the days when they lived together in the now famous Martello tower:

> That the pair were collaborating on an anthology of inscriptions in public lavatories was known in their set and was regarded as a philosophers' *divertissement*.[32]

So it is that Colum's two biographies are experiments on the part of their author. On one hand we have Colum turned researcher, "setting the record straight" about Griffith and giving a creditable attempt to survey the whole of contemporary Irish history; on the other hand, Colum the tale-teller and poet reminiscing about his friend and throwing little pencil-beams of light on one of the most darkly obscure works in literature. The collaboration of the Colums on the latter biography was their second such undertaking, the first being the translation of *Hansel and Gretel*. It is unfortunate that there was not more of such collaboration, for it was a happy one. One hears echoes of the biographies in Colum's *Elegies* and in his Noh plays, which again demonstrate his reminiscence technique and his impressionistic attempts to grasp the essential character from a few illustrative moments.

To readers on both sides of the Atlantic, Padraic Colum's essays are common currency. He has been a regular contributor since early in the century to such periodicals as *Everyman, Commonweal, New Republic, The Nation, Dial, Saturday Review, New Statesman, Catholic World, Dublin Magazine,* and *Theatre Arts Magazine,* and he has published four collections of essays, *My Irish*

Year, The Road Round Ireland, Cross Roads in Ireland, and *A Half-Day's Ride.* Perhaps the term *essays* used in describing these four volumes is a bit too specific, because the selections include stories, folk tales, biographical sketches and poetry as well as historical pieces, literary criticism, general description, political propaganda and comments on the social and economic status of Ireland.

The first book, *My Irish Year,* was the third in a series published by Mills and Boon.[33] Like the other two in the series, *My Italian Year* and *My German Year,* Colum's book was to give a "faithful portrait" of the life of the country, a task for which his qualifications were already fairly well known even in 1912. To accomplish this he attempted to take his reader geographically as well as intellectually "through the length and breadth of Ireland and introduce . . . us to all phases of its social life from the highest to the lowest."[34] Colum has pretty much followed the same aims in *The Road Round Ireland* and *Cross Roads in Ireland* but has expanded his horizons in *A Half-Day's Ride* to include observations on a varied number of unexpected places and situations. He says by way of an introductory essay about Charles Lever's novel, *A Day's Ride:*

> Myself, I have resolved—well, now and again—to break through my habitual round by going to places that my friends don't take me to and by reading books that nobody wants me to read. . . . Possibly I shall write an account of my discoveries. (As if I don't have to!)[35]

A Half-Day's Ride, then, deals with such varied places as Hawaii and the Paris opera in contrast to Colum's earlier three books about "the length and breadth of Ireland."

Even these earlier books have, however, various differences in scope and format. *My Irish Year* later was incorporated into the second two books, but with the happy omission of a great deal of nationalistic propaganda which was dated by the time of the publication of the later books and which in the earlier was tedious at best. One can picture young Colum, with a chance to write about Ireland for a British audience, rolling up his patriotic sleeves and sitting down to right the cumulative ills of seven centuries. Fortunately this is only a part of *My Irish Year*, which includes a varied fabric of stories and descriptive material laid out in a geographical pattern to cover southern Ireland. He apologizes in his introduction for the omissions in this pattern.

> "My Irish Year" is not representative of the whole of Ireland: Catholic and Peasant Ireland only is shown, and this Catholic and Peasant Ireland is localised in a strip of country crossing the Midlands to the West. There is nothing of historic Munster in these pages; nothing of East and South Leinster; nothing of Ulster. . . . The cities, Dublin, Belfast, and Cork, each with its distinctive life and atmosphere, have not been brought into the book.[36]

The Road Round Ireland utilizes much of the same material as *My Irish Year*, but fills in most of the geographical gaps, with sections on Leinster, Munster, Cork and Dublin. This leaves still the northern counties to be explored in some detail in *Cross Roads in Ireland*, along with additional looks at the western and southern portions.

There is a gentle shift in approach as between *My Irish Year* and the later two books. The first relies more heavily upon facts and forthright opinions in the narration of what Ireland is like, while the later books are based primarily upon impressions and generalizations from various vignettes and stories, the whole being more a presentation of the feel of the places described than the facts of its people, topography, and so forth. *My Irish Year* was written primarily for a British audience (though it was published in America by James Pott and Company in 1912) while the latter two books were written principally for an American audience, and included, for instance, such Irish-American portraits as the one of John Devoy, the editor of *The Gaelic American*.

The stories from *My Irish Year*, however, were included with little revision in the later collections, and one, "The Flute-Player's Story," comes to us unscathed from Colum's original volume of stories, *Studies*, published in 1907, through *My Irish Year* to reappear again in *The Road Round Ireland*.

In all three works the style is familiar, folksy and first person. We see the countryside and its people through Colum's eyes and his reactions are ours. The author sometimes lapses from first to third person narration in his story sequences, but always returns to the role of self-appointed observer and commentator. When the narrator launches out into a descriptive passage or story it is always in the present tense, which conveys a feeling of the narrator and reader's presence at an event, but which also is a little disconcerting until one is fully acclimated to it. It is perhaps the most distinctive element in Colum's narrative technique.

On first glance Colum's narrative design seems to have only a random pattern. His descriptions are interspersed with his biographical sketches and miscellaneous pieces with no apparent rationale except the geographical one. In the three Irish books Colum usually gives a general description of the part of the country under consideration and then develops a feeling for its inhabitants through a series of stories, biographies or social or historical commentary about the people who live there. One wonders occasionally if the stories are always indigenous only to the part of the country Colum is dealing with at the time. In at least one case the locale is changed from one book to another while the story remains otherwise intact. One can just see the Munster or Connacht people nodding their respective heads in recollection at various versions of a story entitled "The Death of the Rich Man," in which the description of Connacht in *My Irish Year* becomes that of Munster in *Cross Roads in Ireland*. Following is the quotation from *My Irish Year* with the *Cross Roads in Ireland* variations indicated in brackets:

> It was a road as shelterless and bare as any road in Connacht [Munster]. On one side there was a far-stretching [far-reaching] bog, on the other side little fields, cold

with tracts of water. You faced the Connacht [Comeragh] hills, bleak and treeless, with little streams across them like threads of steel.[37]

Such deceptions are exceptional, however, and throughout the three Irish books Colum maintains a sense of reality in the scenes described. When one tries to infer a time from the descriptions or from the characters, he is left with only a sense of antiquity and timelessness. The scenes are contemporary to the time the book was written; this we can see from the political and social commentary. But the places and the people are not restricted to a particular period, and it is this sense of the changeless in the people and the scene that Colum is able to capture so well.

He does not seek to give a Utopian picture of the people or their lot. There is poverty recorded in his essays, and there are portraits of greed and avarice among his people. For instance, "The Death of the Rich Man," referred to above, is an allegory of human greed as harsh as the one represented in *Thomas Muskerry*. Not all of Colum's stories and characters are grim, however. A Colum Kildare Christmas story, for example, is a very funny parody of the nativity narrative done in an Irish style.

Upon close inspection we perceive that Colum's seemingly meandering presentation actually follows an inductive methodology. He presents a series of character portraits, descriptions, stories and commentary, juxtaposing presidents with peasants and heroes with timid girls, the composite of which suggests the nature of each region. When the fragments fall in place the idea that emerges is the sort of recollection and impression one has when he visits an area and talks to its inhabitants. The sum total of the impressions the author gathers in all of the regions he visits is thus a living sense of Ireland, what it looks like, how it thinks, what it says, and what it really is.

A *Half-Day's Ride*, on the other hand, though it uses the same free association techniques as the other three volumes of essays, presents a picture more of the mind of its author than of a place or country. Without a geographical pattern, this book even more than the other essay volumes is a Charles Lamb-like, leisurely, congenial ramble through the experiences of the author and the implications they had for him, and by extension, all of us. Often these implications are not stated, but just the facts of the experience, such as judging a Miss Europe beauty contest or befriending midgets. In many ways this volume is the best of the essay collections, for in it Colum is unhampered by the restraints imposed by his design in the other books. He is free to conduct a conversation with a cat, to meditate on cakes, and, in short, to invoke the poet's right of choice. Coupled with this is a romantic poet's disdain for the literal facts and his equation of preciseness with pedantry. Occasionally this casualness about fact leads Colum into such deep water as misquoting *Ulysses*,[38] but on the whole if one is caught up in the spirit of the essays there is no problem of credibility.

If the sweet accents of Eire are missing from *A Half-Day's Ride*, Colum finds clumps of the ould sod in other parts of the world, especially in Hawaii. His extensive travel among the Polynesian peoples reveals one basic similarity to the Irish, a similarity that may have been acknowledged by the Polynesians themselves when they chose an Irishman to record their customs and folklore. The sense of great antiquity merging with the contemporary is a part of Colum's Hawaii as well as his Ireland. Throughout *A Half-Day's Ride* he intersperses ancient places with contemporary, out of the way places like Bimini and Moloki with London, New York and Paris, whimsy with practical criticism, and phantasy with logic. His method is unchanged here, but he has expanded his scope to include the whole world.

Colum's literary criticism, counter to what is fashionable today in America, deals more with an author's intent than his method of writing and with overall design rather than with the specifics of a work. His criticism is often a tangent to a portrait of a writer, a portrait done with the insight of a close friend. Even Colum's account of Goldsmith has this sense of the personal and a wariness of the academic approach.

In his political writing his fierce nationalism and his fervor for the unification of Ireland afford us some of his most polemical, easily dated and eminently forgettable prose. Only when it is laced with history does it begin to come alive, and when Colum dwells exclusively on history the interest quotient rises rapidly. He translates the great events of ancient Ireland into simple terms of battles and heroes with the experience of a natural storyteller who sees the events and the people involved as great and wondrous, while his view of contemporary Irish history has all the appeal of a first-hand account by someone who has lived and suffered through it.[39]

Colum's essays contain the germs of several other works to follow. There are segments from *Our Friend James Joyce* and *Ourselves Alone* in both *The Road Round Ireland* and *A Half-Day's Ride*, and Colum's stylistic format in the Joyce biography is the same as he uses in the essays. His design of explicating Ireland through a geographical tour was later put to use in *The Poet's Circuits* and in the recent stage presentation, *Carricknabauna*. His idea of linking great men and ancient places, which forms the pattern of his Noh play cycle, is part of *The Road Round Ireland*, and it is in that book that he first links Roger Casement and Monasterboice.

Colum's essays do not comprise his greatest contribution to literature, but they are certainly central to some of his main literary objectives. His essay collections bring to bear on his central goal of explicating the Gestalt of Ireland his sensibilities as poet, dramatist and novelist, his great historical acumen, his knowledge of people, and his ear for speech. But his essays go beyond this to fantasy, whimsy, humor and a delicious sense of the absurd: those things which make up a great storyteller and writer of children's books. Part of this capability comes through in *A Half-Day's Ride* as does the assurance that Colum is a citizen of the world as well as Ireland. The whole mind of the man is on display in the essays more than any other segment of his work, for they are a collection of all of his several considerable talents, and so it is through the essays that his whole worth begins to be ascertainable. The collections are delightful, penetrating and truthful because they reflect more accurately than any other area of his work the personality of the author.

This chapter through its look at the fiction, biographies and essays of Padraic Colum, if nothing else, indicates the broad scope of his interest and accomplishment. Colum has tried his hand at all of the various forms of writing, and even his friend, James Joyce, could not have boasted of being as successful in so many media.

As the patterns of Colum's prose become apparent we are able to see certain tendencies running throughout the material discussed in this chapter: First, his penchant for defining, describing, analyzing, and illuminating his country. Through the speech which he captures with such accuracy, through his vivid descriptions and through his lifelike characterization, the Ireland of the late nineteenth and twentieth centuries comes alive in his novels, biographies and essays. Relaxed familiarity coupled with humor and first person present tense narration make his style both distinctive and easy to read. This ease of comprehension tends, as in the case of his poetry, to belie the intricacy of structure and design in his novels and to underscore the portrait of the unassuming author in his essays.

5

Children's Literature

Colum's children's literature, like his other work, appears to be uncomplex and perhaps even accidental, while it is in reality the thoughtful product of a skilled craftsman, long practiced in his art and knowing exactly the kinds of results he wishes to achieve. In this final area of discussion we see that all of the tendencies which are so prevalent in his poetry, drama and narrative will combine in his children's literature to make Colum's books classics in the field. His directness and simplicity, his eye for descriptions and ear for dialogue, his ability to capture the atmosphere of a scene, and his great love of Ireland and its countryside are all contributing factors to the excellence of his children's literature.

Colum's remarkable booklet, *Story Telling New and Old*, reveals the priorities and techniques that have made his children's literature some of the best and most popular ever published in the United States. In the area of children's books, where the criteria for judgment are different from adult fiction, popular success or the lack of it is a prime requisite in the evaluation of any work. In short, the work must be interesting to the children for whom it is intended, rather than merely to an elite group of intellectuals or critics who dictate the trends. It is signficant that in *Story Telling New and Old* Colum stresses the oral style, because the dominant element in his children's prose is a sense of its being told aloud by a storyteller. If Colum often stretches credibility to establish a single narrator-speaker for a whole series of unrelated stories, he does it to achieve this atmosphere of the storyteller beside the turf fire, the attitude which had made such an indelible impression on him as a child.

Colum's storyteller is informal in his approach and diction but never condescending. Citing Walter Scott's statement that children love stories that are intended for their betters, Colum tells us in his booklet:

> The story-teller must have respect for the child's mind and the child's conception of the world, knowing it for a complete mind and a complete conception. If a story-teller have that respect he need not be childish in his language in telling stories to children. If the action be clear and the sentences clear one can use a mature language. Strange words, out-of-the-way words do not bewilder children if there be order in the action and in the sentences. They like to hear such words.[1]

Since Colum never condescends or talks down to his audience, the question inevitably arises whether his children's books are really children's books at all. Would they not be perfectly acceptable for adults? When I put the question to him, his reply evoked his own experiences in childhood.

> If you sat in a house the children would be listening to the man who would be telling the story, but so would the adults. They [the stories] are children's in the sense that they would be told very simply and straightforwardly, and they are about wonders, which children like. But who is to say what a children's story is.[2]

Nevertheless, the stories are intended for children: the really sensual passages in the mythology, especially the Polynesian mythology, have been muted. Colum acknowledges the elimination of some sex, war, and blood, but retains other equally realistic passages when they are an integral part of the narrative. He refuses, however, to write moralistic literature.

> It is more important to let a child's imagination develop than it is to labor to inculcate in him or her some correct ethical point of view.[3]

His legends often tend to follow basic formulas of action and motifs, and rely heavily on wonders and marvels. The ritual phrases and formula actions are not the result of imaginative drought; they are essential to the way Colum feels a storyteller should operate.

> It would be well if the modern and metropolitan storyteller could do what that story-teller's art permitted him to do—to make certain descriptions purely conventional —the description of a ship sailing the sea, for instance; the description of a castle or of a lonely waste. . . . When he set his ship sailing upon the sea, when he set this hero wandering through a wilderness, the audience rested and the story-teller rested, not because there was nothing happening, but because what was happening was regular and anticipated.[4]

I have adopted Macmillan's rather arbitrary division of the types of Colum's children's books as the format of my discussion.[5] Under the title "World Epics" are included epical stories and mythology, under "Folk Romance," Colum's purely legendary and romantic stories, and under "Stories for Younger Children," the rest of the Colum children's canon. I have referred to Macmillan's division as arbitrary because in Colum's manner of telling them, many of the epics lose the grandeur and scope of the epical style that scholars try so diligently to preserve, and they are reduced to the category of romantic tales. Further the simplicity with which Colum tells the stories underscores the fact that they are all really folk romances—epical, mythological or not. Finally, when we examine the stories supposedly intended for little children we find that the same stories have a wide appeal for older children and adults.

Some sort of classification is needed, however, if we are to get a perspective of the scope and quality of Colum's children's books, and the Macmillan division seems to afford that, if for no other reason than that it indicates the markets for which the books were intended.

Six works fall into the "World Epics" category: *The Children's Homer, The Golden Fleece, The Children of*

Odin, The Island of the Mighty, The Voyagers, and *Orpheus.*

Colum is quite candid about his eminent reputation as a folklorist and mythologist.

> The mythologists and folklorists would disclaim that I had any knowledge of [mythology]. After all I'm not a folklorist and I'm not a mythologist and shouldn't be compared with a real folklorist in the field . . . I began by telling the stories I remembered from my grandmother's house in *The King of Ireland's Son* and then I was labeled as a folklorist and mythologist and I went in with it. If they asked if I'd write a book about folklore . . . why I wrote it. I didn't get it wrong you know—I looked it up and consulted the authorities in the libraries and so on. I don't undertake things that I'm not able to do, though my wife was always accusing me of that.

> But then I kept on reading it of course. I was interested in folklore and mythology and I kept on reading it. But the idea of my setting myself up as a folklorist or a mythologist is nonsense. I didn't set myself up, but the Hawaiian legislature thought I was the man. [cf., p. 15] The main thing was my ability to write these stories and an interest in them. After all you could get a real field worker in folklore who couldn't do that and would be less good to them.[6]

Typically, Colum understates his research in the preparation of his manuscripts. Lionel Trilling, in one of the few critical analyses of Colum's children's literature, finds Colum's treatment of Greek epics complete and accurate.[7] If Colum is not technically an expert, he has certainly done his homework well, and in his translations of the myths, folklore, and epics he is, as he says, better able to tell the stories to his prospective audience than more serious but less gifted scholars. Though this audience ostensibly consisted of children, I doubt if his style and manner of telling the epics would have been greatly modified if they had been intended for adult consumption. Some things might have been changed or added— for instance, Achilles' treatment of Hector's body in *The*

Children's Homer might not have been glossed over as quickly as Colum has done—but for the most part Colum retains much of the violence of both the *Iliad* and the *Odyssey*.

His longest book of mythology, *Orpheus, Myths of the World,* has a lengthy preface detailing in a scholarly fashion the background of the various myths. Colum acknowledges that the book was not principally intended for juvenile readers: "*Orpheus* is not for children. *Orpheus* is for students of mythology who want a ready reference book." [8] Yet many of the stories in *Orpheus* had already been published by Colum in other children's books.

Perhaps because the epics and mythology of the Greeks are the most familiar of the world's legends to Colum and his prospective audience, *The Children's Homer* and *The Golden Fleece* were the first and the most popular of the children's epics. *The Children's Homer* appeared in 1918 and was republished in 1946 and 1962 by Macmillan in New York and in 1920 in London. *The Golden Fleece,* appearing in 1921, was also republished twice more, in 1957 and 1962. The tremendous popularity of these books is due simply to the fact that they are the best translations for children available of these epics. Lionel Trilling compares Hawthorne's version of the Greek classics for children with Colum's, concluding that Hawthorne's translation must have been intended for girls, such was his language and demeanor, while Colum's retains the realism of the original and is not nearly so condescending. There is no heavy moral theme in Colum's work as in Hawthorne but a clear, ungilded rendition of the tale as close to the original as possible. Thus the direct style which has been the touchstone of all of Colum's books, from the poetry through the essays, comes into its most utilitarian phase here. There was no need for Colum to adopt a new style when he wrote for children, since children's literature demands exactly the sort of simplicity with which Colum has invested everything he wrote. However, simplicity does not imply a lack of variety in his narrative method. For example, in *The Children's Homer* there is a strong biblical influence. As Telemachus leaves Ithaca in search of his father, Colum writes a Genesis-like beginning for the tale which is to follow:

> And now they set up the mast of pine and they made it fast with forestays, and they hauled up the sails with ropes of twisted oxhide. And a wind came and filled out the sails, and the youths pulled at the oars, and the ship dashed away.[9]

There are traces of formal, archaic language in all Colum's epical works, especially in the dialogue of Gods and in the phraseology describing ritualistic events.

> In the morning they feasted and did sacrifice, and when he had given judgments to the people, the old King Nestor spoke to his sons:
> "Lo, now, my sons. Yoke for Telemachus the horses to the chariot that he may go his way to Sparta." [10]

The simplicity of the narrative style lies not so much in easy words as in a lack of complexity in syntax and sentence construction. The words themselves are very often the sort that children, especially younger children, might have to look up. *The Voyagers* especially employs a fairly advanced vocabulary for children. Of course, most of the tales in *The Voyagers* are related by a storyteller native to the country of the story's origin, and so the narrative point of view in the book appears quite adult.

The several books in this children's epic series show differences in format and intent as well as style. *The Children's Homer* takes its format from the *Odyssey*, with the action of the *Iliad* occurring in the form of a narrative by Menelaus and Helen. Of course Colum's version makes no pretense of substituting for an adult version of Homer. The pride of Odysseus, his guile and dissemblance, the very qualities that over the centuries have made him such an absorbing character to mature audiences, are gone, as is the childish peevishness of

Achilles, and such epic trappings as the roll call of the troops before Troy. Yet the narrative retains most of its wonder and spectacle, and these are the things which interest children. The questions of fate, *hubris*, and motivation, so urgent to instructors in Great Books courses, are hardly apparent to the reader of *The Children's Homer*, nor should they be, any more than corruption in government or the degeneracy of man should occur as issues to the youngster reading *Gulliver's Travels*. Colum has included only those elements that would make the story memorable for the young reader. His omission of segments tangential to the narrative, has indeed restricted its epical quality, but this has been replaced by the essential and primitive quality of the folk ballad, a characteristic which was to fit so well the folk material of his other great children's books.

As is suggested by the complete title of Colum's second book of Greek epics, *The Golden Fleece and the Heroes Who Lived Before Achilles*, the narrative contains more than a single plot line. Colum skillfully interweaves Jason and the Argonauts' search for the Golden Fleece with a description of the several adventures of the heroes who made up the crew of the Argo. To organize the tangential material Colum again uses his favorite device, that of the external narrator, this time mainly Orpheus, who emerges from *The Golden Fleece* looking a good deal like an old Irish harper or the traveling poet of *Poet's Circuits*. The tangents are at moments disconcerting, but only because Colum's narrative of the Golden Fleece itself is so compacted as to be free from most of the extraneous material originally contained in the Greek tale. The tangential material also includes a five page history encompassing the period from the origin of the world through the overthrow of the Titans, so that *The Golden Fleece* seems more mythological than does *The Children's Homer*, though the language of *The Golden Fleece* contains fewer archaisms.

Between his volumes of Greek epics Colum published a book of Scandinavian myths and epics, *The Children of Odin,* successful enough to demand five subsequent editions or reissuings, including one in Irish translation. The first sections of the book are devoted to the Gods at Asgard, the second and third parts to Odin and other wandering immortals, and the last section to the Volsung epics, with a final six page twilight for the Gods. The tales are far less bloodthirsty than the Greek epics, but there are a fair share of dragons and so forth, and a few moments of stark realism in the Volsung section, such as the scene in which Signy sews Sigmund's gloves to his hands and Sigmund subsequently demonstrates his manliness by removing the gloves and stripping off his skin. The mythological parts, with their dwarfs and elves, are invested by Colum with a sort of fairy tale atmosphere and a sense that he enjoys them a good deal more than the stronger, realistic material.

The legend of the sword of the Volsungs has come to us in popular form through the emotional music of Wagner, but Colum too has managed to catch the epic passion of Brynhild even with his sparseness and simplicity of story line. This story, at least for me, is the high point of the book, much more meaningful than the household affairs and mischief of the Gods. The romances of Sigmund and Sigurd achieve an inherent dramatic quality which renders them unique in the hands of a storyteller like Colum.

Colum's only other volume wholly devoted to the epical stories of a single people or religion is *The Island of the Mighty,* which comprises the heroic stories of Celtic Britain retold from *The Mabinogion.* The tales deal with heroes rather than Gods, so they could more properly be described as romances rather than mythology. Unless one reads the introduction carefully, he is mildly jarred by such elevated descriptions as the following:

> There is a castle on a lofty mountain, and there is a maiden therein, and she is detained a prisoner there, and whoever shall set her free will attain the summit of the fame of the world.[11]

It is comforting to learn in the introduction, however, that the prose of the volume sampled above is not Colum's at all but that of Lady Charlotte Guest. Colum's contribution was editorial in *The Island of the Mighty*. He selected and edited stories from *The Mabinogion* and rearranged them, leaving them in Guest's prose. He later made his own translations of selected myths from *The Mabinogion* for inclusion in *Orpheus*. The stories are important in the sense that the youthful protagonists of Colum's own two novels were patterned after the young heroes of *The Mabinogion*. He might be describing his own protagonists when he tells us, "In these stories we seem to see immortal youth moving through a world that knows no change or decay." [12] The stories had the added attraction for Colum of being part of a background common to both the Irish and the Welsh. He also edited *Gulliver's Travels* and the *Arabian Nights* for the children but never considered them so much his own as he did *The Island of the Mighty*.

The Voyagers combines Colum's own prose with factual reports of explorers on the several journeys to the New World. The stories are told in clear vigorous prose which bows to stylistic idiosyncrasies only in the accounts purported to have been written by the explorers themselves. The voyages of Maelduin and Saint Brenden are the most extensive accounts and are really epical in nature, with Saint Brenden's search for "The Radiant Land" taking on marked aspects of the spiritual journey allegory as well. As Colum moves through the Viking narratives toward the story of the discovery of America, the prose becomes leaner and the accounts much more interesting and romantic, reaching a climax as Ponce de Leon is slain by an arrow just as he tastes his first sip of water from the Fountain of Youth. The historical accounts, invested with truth by their original authors, and with romance and suspense by Colum, form an exciting second half to the book.

Orpheus: Myths of the World was commissioned by Macmillan and was not undertaken for the mere love of storytelling, as some of the other books were. Colum confines himself to myths in this, the largest of his collections, restricting his definition of the term and hence the scope of the book.

> Mythology is made up of stories regarded as sacred that form an integral and active part of a culture. The stories in this collection will be such, or they will have the marks of having been at one time such.[13]

Hence Odysseus, Achilles and Jason have no part in Colum's anthology, while Prometheus, Dionysus and Heracles do.

If, as Colum says, the book was intended as a scholarly publication, there are obvious reasons why it missed the mark. First, it made no pretense of completeness. Each of the seventeen civilizations is represented by from one to eight tales, ranging in size from a couple of paragraphs to seventeen pages. Obviously *Orpheus* represents only a random sampling of the world's mythology, and no matter how clearly and simply the stories are told, the book could not be considered an indispensable text in its field. Then, too, Mr. Colum's sense of artistic integrity has led him into some very unscholarly practices such as making up part of the second Egyptian myth to give the narrative line continuity. If there is an occasion for difference between the aesthetic and the scholarly—and there are several in *Orpheus*—Colum always, quite understandably, chooses artistry. This is perfectly legitimate, but of course it will not sell textbooks. Colum originally wrote the book under a commission which was supposed to provide him with a fairly steady income over the years. The fact that it has not is due in part to the fact that Colum has produced a book which is too imaginative for the serious student of mythology and too scholarly for children.

Colum's Hawaiian books resemble his other volumes of mythology in their manner of presentation. They are his only children's books which are not illustrated profusely, though there are brief illustrations at the beginning of each tale in *Legends of Hawaii*. This book, the third in the series, published by Yale University Press, is a collection of selected legends drawn from the preceding two, with the addition of some new material.

Colum derived the bulk of the material in the three volumes from John Wise's translation of the collection of Hawaiian folklore gathered by Abraham Fornander during the middle of the nineteenth century. Mr. Fornander collected the manuscripts representing the surviving tradition of Hawaii with the help of a corps of native scholars, and on his death in 1887 the collection was acquired by Charles R. Bishop. It later became a permanent holding of the Bishop Museum of Polynesian Ethnology and Natural History in Honolulu. The manuscripts, together with the translations, were subsequently published by the Bishop Museum. Colum's commission from the Hawaiian Legislature was to remake the stories into coherent, interesting stories for children in the Hawaiian schools. In order to do this he decided to steep himself in as much Hawaiian background as he could.

> I made it my main task to understand the background of the stories given in that collection, and to hear as many of them as possible from the lips of the surviving custodians of the Polynesian tradition in Hawaii.[14]

Colum completely reshaped many of the older stories to fit into a narrative pattern he found workable.

> I have had to condense, expand, heighten, subdue, rearrange—in a word, I have had to retell the stories, using the old romances as material for wonder-stories. The old stories were not for children; they gave an image of life to kings and soldiers, to courtiers and to ruling women. As in all stories not originally intended for children, much has had to be suppressed in retelling them for a youthful audience.
>
> And retelling them has meant that I have had to find a new form for the stories. The form that I choose to give them is that of the European folk-tale.[15]

Thus, Colum transformed Hawaii's legends and myths into the kind of tales he had been telling all along. There were certain differences in characters and activities, as the dragons of Europe became octopi and the jousting gave way to surfing. The stories seem a great deal more sensual than those Europeans tell within earshot of their children, but Colum manages to marry off most of the lovers or render their activities mild enough to pass his Irish conscience. Still, the sexual freedom which is part of the Polynesian culture is still very much a part of the background of these tales.

All through the legends there is a feeling for nature which is indigenous to the tales themselves rather than to Colum's rendition of them. The scenes and descriptions are lush, and much of the substance of the legends deals directly with natural surroundings rather than human or even animal manifestations. The stories have a great deal of miraculous activity in them that is not of the sort one normally expects in folktales; for example, in "The Seven Deeds of Ma-ui," the boy fishes up an entire island out of the sea, holds up the sky, and performs similar acts. With the exception of Ma-ui the heroes are not heroes in the classical sense of the term: men who set out specifically to do such impossible feats as finding the Golden Fleece. Rather the Polynesian heroes seem to be no more than local boys, not exceptionally gifted, who are fortunate enough to come by the wherewithal to perform exceptional deeds.

The legends often depict the pathos of common people and their difficult tasks in life. For example, "Hina, the Woman of the Moon," is the story of a woman worn down by toil who goes to rest on the moon via a rainbow. As she attempts to mount the rainbow her husband grabs her leg and cripples her. In such stark strokes the story catches with folk ballad-like economy the hardships of everyday life. The details are omitted but the fervency of the woman's longing indicates the extent of her suffering.

Some of the European formulas such as the Cinderella motif still remain, and day to day life goes on as sharks are slain and maidens won. Colum's need, real or fan-

cied, to tie all the tales in a given volume into one
continuous narrative framework is missing here, so that
each story stands alone as a separate entity. It could
hardly have been otherwise with source material so variegated.

> These stories are of different types: some are folk tales,
> stories told to and by unlearned people from time imme-
> morial and some are stories told by learned men to a
> cultivated audience, court romances comparable, although
> they are not in verse, to the lays made by minstrels for the
> medieval courts of Europe.[16]

Despite their differences Colum invests the legends
with the magic of his own storytelling techniques: he
adds poetry and his attitude of a kindly storyteller relating to children the lore of their heritage.

> Light it now. One ku-kui nut and then another will burn
> along the string as I tell my stories. It is well that you have
> brought so many nuts, my younger brother.[17]

With Colum, folklore is all one piece and children are
children. In the Hawaiian legends the only difference is
that the pieces of turf for the fire have become ku-kui
nuts.

Colum's first Hawaiian volume, *At the Gateways of
the Day*, consists principally of legendary material, while
the second, *The Bright Islands*, contains a large section
of history, slightly modified by the author.

> This section is made up of chronicles, but chronicles that
> have taken on a legendary tinge through being passed on
> by oral historians. Naturally, in reshaping the histories of
> Moi-keha, Umi, Ka-welo, and Ka-meha-meha, I have
> made more of the legendary than of the literal happen-
> ings.[18]

This is not to say that the book lacks its share of the
miraculous and the romantic. But here the emphasis is
on a history of Hawaiian kings and battles rather than
the little people of the other legends.

Since Colum prefers the legendary rather than the

historical, it is only natural that *Legends of Hawaii,* a collection of the two preceding volumes, should derive most of its material from *At the Gateways of the Day* and add a few more tales and legends which are not basically historical. As in his other republished works he makes frequent changes from the original, this time producing slightly less formal and stilted narrative. Together the three volumes represent a brief but important period for their author. The recognition that was afforded his work by the request from the Hawaiian Legislature gave him new stature in the world of children's literature, and the assimilation of a whole body of material alien, but in a way similar to the folk stories he had known, were later to bear fruit in other endeavors in world mythology such as *Orpheus.* Colum had arrived as an eminent children's writer. The Hawaiian books complete Colum's mythology cycle, the extent and scope of which have earned him an international reputation as an expert on myths. However, it is not his scholarly posture in the field which has attracted world attention but his unfailing genius for translating the myths he deals with into delightful stories for children.

Macmillan's second category of Colum's children's books, "Folk Romance," encompasses both legendary and popular romantic material. I have included Macmillan's third category, "Stories for Younger Children," in this section and redivided the stories into three groups with the following designations: a) Irish Folklore and Legend, b) Miscellaneous Collections of Tales, c) Longer Single Narratives.

In the first of these categories, there are four volumes of Irish tales, legends, and stories for children. They are *The King of Ireland's Son, The Big Tree of Bunlahy, The Legend of Saint Columba,* and *The Frenzied Prince.*

The first three books contain legends and stories of ancient Ireland, while *The Big Tree of Bunlahy* is a mixture of tales about all phases of Irish life. The narratives, which range from ghost stories to soap opera, are all told in the highly stylized fashion which Colum gives to his more freely adapted and recited books. We know that his descriptions will be free-wheeling from the very first paragraph:

> Bunlahy calls itself a village, but it isn't a village at all. What is it, then? Just a single row of houses facing a wall that shuts in the wood and pasture belonging to an old, deserted mansion. If there were two rows of houses, one facing the other, it might have the right to call itself a village. But there never was, and there never will be, two rows of houses in Bunlahy. And yet it is because Bunlahy has but the one row of houses (and you might count them on the fingers of your hands) that it got part of the great fame that it has.[19]

The style represents Colum at his playful best. The Irish irreverence, one of the hallmarks of his best loved prose works, is too often lost in his close translations of the epics and myths, but finds its full flowering in stories in which he has no one particular clearly delineated source to which he feels he must adhere. Happily for the book, *The Big Tree of Bunlahy* is a collection of just such stories. There is the familiar first person narration, with several storytellers relating their tales to the central character. The range of the tales, unlike those in Colum's other books, is unlimited and so is the author's imagination.

The other three Irish books deal chiefly in ancient romantic lore about impossible deeds and comely maidens to be rescued and married. The first and best of these books is *The King of Ireland's Son*, the book upon which Colum's initial reputation as a children's author was made. Its success depends more on informality than any other single factor. The playfulness previously mentioned is part of the technique in *The King of Ireland's Son*, used with special effectiveness in the animal fables, where talking beasts can be just as impudent as humans.

In addition, Colum's humor often takes the form of a series of adjectives so impressive that what follows seems anticlimactic, as in the following example: "He got off the bob-tailed, big-headed, spavined, and spotted horse, and came in." [20] Furthermore, the names of Colum's characters and animals are usually long and very often repeated.

> "Go your own way now, my Slight Red Steed."
> When he said that the Slight Red Steed twitched its ears and galloped toward the West. . . . He jumped off the Slight Red Steed, pushed the door of the house open, and there, seated on a chair in the middle of the floor with a woman sitting beside him, was the Enchanter of the Black Backlands. "So," said the Enchanter, "my Slight Red Steed has brought you to me." [21]

All of these devices generate an undercurrent of humor which runs throughout the book and in fact through most good children's books. The humor seldom surfaces long or obviously enough to cause real hilarity, but its presence is always felt just below the surface, reassuring the young reader that there is equanimity in the world and that things will eventually be all right, no matter how bad they seem at the time. Such an attitude is important to youngsters, and the best children's works convey it. *The King of Ireland's Son* radiates a kind of smugness in accepting the incredible, which, it is implied, mundane adults would be incapable of understanding. The book abounds in such little parenthetical confidences as the following:

> (all cats know men's language, but men do not know that the cats know). He told them not to be too haughty (as a king might be inclined to be) to any creature in the Forge. [22]

The first confidence, which is incredible, is juxtaposed with the much more believable one following, so that the first seems more a mundane, everyday truth and the second miraculous by association. This technique, reminiscent of Lewis Carroll, is common to Colum's best children's books, in which he does not adhere too closely to already existing translations, or slavishly follow someone else's text. In *The King of Ireland's Son* he allows

himself much more freedom of style and creates a playful attitude which makes the book delightful reading.
The more Colum puts of himself into his children's
books the better they are.

The King of Ireland's Son, founded loosely upon Irish
legend and folk material, is constructed mainly upon two
narratives, those of the king's son and Flann, another
prince who later turns out to be a brother to the first.
Along the boys' routes to ultimate bliss, there are animal
fables, mock epics, religious allegories, poems, and fairy
tales, with overtones of England and the Irish revolution
throughout. The book concludes with a Dickensian sort
of unraveling in which everyone knows, or is related to,
everyone else and the pieces of the two narratives fall
neatly into place. The King of Ireland's Son's search for
his love, Fedelma, in the first half of the book gives way
in the second to Flann's search for his identity, the
theme which flowered in Colum's later novels. But if
The King of Ireland's Son lacks the lofty purpose and
design of the later novels, it more than compensates in
its appeal to its own particular audience and in its high
spirited style.

The Frenzied Prince and The Legend of Saint Columba come late in the Colum canon of children's stories. The action of these two books of Irish legend is
more serious and restrained than the book just discussed.
They have in common the concern with ancient Irish
legendary, romantic, heroic material.

The principal differences between the two books lie
in structure and narrative setting. The Frenzied Prince is
a loose collection of tales told to a seemingly mad prince
to keep him from beating his head against the walls.
Included in the tales are the stories of two of Ireland's
most popular heroes, Finn MacCuhal and Cuchullain.
These stories are as exciting as any in the Colum canon,
as is the tale of Prince Suivne, the Frenzied Prince.
Many of the stories of the heroes are little more than
fairy tales, but others are loaded with real adventure and
realistic detail, especially in the Cuchullain cycle. The

legends are traditional, such as the story of how the harp came to Tara, and their treatment by Colum is understated and engaging.

One factor setting *The Frenzied Prince* apart from Colum's other Irish books for children is the beautiful physical layout of the book. Willy Pogany, who did the illustrations for many of Colum's children's books, was given license to do full color and charcoal illustrations instead of the line drawings in the Macmillan volumes. *The Frenzied Prince* was published by the David McKay Company on what must have been a more lavish budget, for the drawings are abundant and the type is set in several sizes to reflect whether each tale is a part of the narrative framework or one of the interwoven stories. The book is the handsomest, if not the best, of Colum's works.

The Legend of Saint Columba is in comparison remarkably unified. Except for a few detours, the book is a compact history of the Saint's life and trials. His miracles and feats are occasionally blended with stories of ghosts and fairies, which are charming even if they add no great dignity to the legend. The narrative, like so many others, is neither really a children's nor an adults' story. A mixture of Christian journeys and Irish national history, the book provides the saint with enough human weakness and humanity to render him very often a touching figure. But someone who can command the natural elements to obey his bidding is hardly an object of much pity and fear for the reader. Rather Saint Columba's or Colum-cille's adventures are far too mundane to compete with the action packed careers of epic heroes, and his portrait is too realistically drawn—with his faults clearly displayed—for him to achieve the traditional heroic role. However, there is something of an "epical" novel in *The Legend of Saint Columba* with a strain of fidelity to historical fact. Accounts like those of the search for the master poem of Ireland seem reminiscent of the light-hearted search for "The Unique Tale" in *The King of Ireland's Son*, but the intent here is vastly different. There is an underlying reverence for Irish religion and history which gives the story a serious cast. While the book does not provide as much pleasure as Colum's first children's narrative of Irish heroes, it still contains a wide range of ancient material both Christian and pagan and is valuable to both adults and children for its history, poetry, and legend.

Colum wrote twelve other books for children which were based on general European folklore and his own invention. One, *Six Who Were Left in a Shoe*, published by Brentano in 1924, was never bound or seen in the United States,[23] and two others, *The Fountain of Youth* and *The Stone of Victory*, are collections of earlier stories which are included elsewhere in this survey. The others may be divided into the two groups previously referred to: "Miscellaneous Collections of Tales," and "Longer Single Narratives." The first group, consisting of *The Boy Who Knew What the Birds Said*, *The Forge in the Forest*, and *The Peep-Show Man*, are all collections of tales while the second group consists of one simple plot and narrative line.

Practically all of the books contain a sprinkling of poetry and the familiar device of the oral storyteller. All of the books are recommended for younger children as contrasted with *The Children's Homer* and *The Golden Fleece*, for instance, which were switched in the 1950's from H. G. Wilson's *Children's Catalogue* to *The Junior High School Catalogue*.[24] Two of the books, *The Peep-Show Man* and *The White Sparrow*, are for very young children, while the rest are intended for youngsters of grade school age.

Like many of the other tales, *The Boy Who Knew What the Birds Said* is memorable not so much for its content, which is predictably miraculous fare, but for the fantastic premise on which it is based, and this understated in the most casual, brief terms imaginable:

> There is one thing that all the Birds are afraid of, and that is the thing that will happen when the Bird That Follows the Cuckoo flies into the Cuckoo's mouth.

> And what will happen then, asks my kind foster-child.
> When the Bird that Follows the Cuckoo flies into the
> Cuckoo's mouth the World will come to an end.[25]

When the Boy covers the Cuckoo's head, thus prevent-
ing the Bird That Follows the Cuckoo from flying in, he
earns the good fortune of understanding bird talk. Colum's use of capital letters in proper names and the
length of the names of his characters and creatures point
up the basic humor which underlies and gives a special
flavor to all his stories for children. His hyphenated
appellations sometimes go on for lines, and some of his
characters act under a number of aliases, such as Cinderella, who is variously known as The-Girl-Who-Sat-by-the-
Ashes, Girl-Go-With-the-Goats, Maid-Alone, Matchless
Maiden, and Brown Girl.

The Forge in the Forest contains eight tales in all, two
each about fire, water, earth and air. The scope of the
tales is large, including stories of Greek mythology as
well as biblical and folk legend. They are set in some
highly stylized illustrations by Boris Artzybasheff, the
same artist who illustrated *Orpheus*. His color drawings
are impressionistic, strong and wild with an appeal as
much to an adult audience as to children. *The Peep-
Show Man*, on the other hand, is a small book for small
children. It contains only three stories, the first being the
Peep-Show Man's own, and the last having a resem-
blance to a Disney picture in which humans and animals
converse.

The last group of children's books to be considered are
those with a single plot line and narrative format. They
might be called novels for children. This is especially
true of the first book that Colum wrote for children, *A
Boy in Eirinn* (1913). There is a marked similarity between this book and the later adult novels, *Castle Conquer* and *The Flying Swans*, but the child's book is
obviously an apprentice piece. *A Boy in Eirinn* was supposed to have been a book designed to depict for American youngsters the life of a typical child in Ireland, but
Colum's patriotism keeps it from completely fulfilling

this intention. The representative Irish boy, Finn O'Donnell, lives with his grandparents because his father is in an English jail for organizing a league for farmers unjustly evicted from their homes, and Finn's mother has gone to America to work. So Colum represents the "typical" Irish boy's life. The piece is, of course, pure propaganda, which the young Colum had to get out of his system before he could begin to write the stories later to win him his reputation as a children's author. Also the book is hardly strengthened by its preface, which takes the form of a letter to the youthful audience from Florence Converse, the general editor of the series. The beginning will suffice to sample that horrendous document:

> Dear Little Schoolmate: —
> If only it were recess, and you and I and five or six other children were playing together, what a good time we should have! [26]

However, A Boy in Eirinn was favorably received, and the book went through seven editions by 1935, with Colum adding a chapter "to bring the book up to date" showing the men that the boys grew up to be. Finn becomes an engineer, building factories in the new industrialized Ireland, with his companion, Tim, a lieutenant in the new Irish army. With the years the book lost none of its propagandistic tendencies. One can see the makings of Castle Conquer in the plot line, the propaganda and the tacked-on ending. But if Colum's later faults appear here, so do the sources of excellence in his later works. The descriptions of the countryside, the house and fireside are detailed, realistic and authentic. One can feel the atmosphere of the country and the city of Dublin. There is much interesting incidental history depicted by the deft pen of a born storyteller. Despite its flaws the book does convey the sense of what it is like to be a child, and one cannot help but feel in reading A Boy in Eirinn that its author, once his mistakes were corrected, had the making of a first-rate children's writer.

In *The Children Who Followed the Piper* and *The Girl Who Sat by the Ashes* Colum reworks the "Pied Piper of Hamlin" and the "Cinderella" stories into longer, greatly improved narratives. The first story deals generally with what happens to the youngsters, especially three of their number, once they follow the piper out of town. In Colum's version some, at least, have reached puberty, for there is a love interest and eventual marriage between two of them. Colum combines mythology, nursery rhymes and folk legend in his tale. The piper is Hermes, with Circe and Mars taking part also in the festivities. The children, with the exception of the three protagonists, are all nursery rhyme characters who do little more than act out their respective rhymes while the protagonists go through the usual folk tale ritual quests.

In *The Girl Who Sat by the Ashes* Colum's contribution to the Cinderella fable is not so much an addition as a transformation. The wicked stepmother, no less wicked, gets a job as the Prince's stewardess to supervise not one but three balls during which the Prince will pick his bride. The happiest change is the representation of the Prince, whom most of us never liked anyway, into an arrogant class-conscious young bigot who has to undergo some humiliation in order to win his love. The Colum treatment is an example of how the author's magic can transform the best known story into something new and interesting.

One of the best of all Colum's single narrative books for young children is *The Boy Apprenticed to an Enchanter*, which takes us on a tour of the Near East and the British Isles, as the boy, after foiling the wicked Enchanter's plot to seize control of Babylon, must flee the Enchanter and seek Merlin, whose magic is greater. In this Wizard-of-Oz type plot there is a good deal of humor provided by the psychological problems of the King as well as the domestic problems of Merlin. If the quest motif with its recurrent cycles of three is standard folk romance, its characters such as Chiron and the Centaur and its occasional poems, humor, and suspense lift it out of a stereotype into something alive and exciting for children.

The two final books to be discussed in this survey, *The White Sparrow* and *Where the Wind Never Blew and the Cocks Never Crew*, are both stories for very young children. *The White Sparrow* is certainly the best of Colum's books for pre-school children, perhaps because it best exemplifies the things that adults like too. Through the birds Colum pokes fun at the stuffiness of humanity. The beginning of the book sets the tone of haughtiness:

> Europe is the center of the world; France is the center of Europe; Paris is the center of France. All of us know this. But not all of us remember that the Luxembourg Gardens are the center of Paris, and the Medici Fountain is the very center of the Luxembourg Gardens. And in the center of the Medici Fountain, just above where the statue of the River God is stooping over the two figures that are just above the water, there is a sparrow's nest.
>
> It is in a very important place, and the owner of it thought of himself as a very important member of the sparrow community.[27]

Colum, who must have been a careful observer of birds' behavior, utilizes the poet's eye for detail in the story, as he perfectly catches the birds' mannerisms as they go about their day to day life.

The story is one of the very few in his books to be wholly the author's own. He sounds jubilant about its originality in his dedication to Mary and Sarah Ann Moore. After having berated them for always telling him that they have heard his stories before, he concludes the passage, "Well, here is one that gives you no chance of triumphing over me. You have never heard it before . . . neither from myself nor anyone else." [28]

The story follows the ugly duckling motif with the difference between the protagonist and the other sparrows being his whiteness. But this story has no magical transformation to swanhood. If anything it is a domestic *bildungsroman* of the feathered community, where the sparrow attends family reunions, learns how to get along in the world, chooses his mate and settles down happy forever after in the elephant statue's mouth in front of the Trocadéro Museum. It is packed with Colum's insight into human activities and ideas, as these are exhibited in the birds, who hardly ever pay any attention to what the other birds are saying, try to shield their offspring from nasty chirping and visit their relatives at least once a year. The story, couched in terms that are as meaningful to adults as to children, is a fine example of the warmth and sensitivity of its author.

Where the Winds Never Blew and the Cocks Never Crew is again for the very young. Basically the day-to-day adventures of domestic animals on a country farm, the book provides a number of familiar didactic messages, such as accepting outsiders, as well as some realistic touches. These extend to a somewhat surprising finish, in which instead of living happily ever after, the animals slowly drift away to die.

> Where did Croodie [the pigeon] go to? She went where all the others had gone—across the edge of the world, where the forefathers of all the pigeons, and of all the guinea hens, and of all the wrens; of all the geese and the crows, the cats and goats and dogs are, and where they never see their shadows.[29]

All that remain are the cat and cricket, who go off to find another old woman and another farm house to live in. The end is quite sober for children and reflects the tendency in Colum's work to treat his readers with the respect that so many other children's authors deny them.

And so Padraic Colum's books for children come full cycle from the mythology, which seems intended neither specifically for adults nor children, to his stories for the youngest children, stories which sound strangely adult in their insights and conclusions. The techniques which characterize his poetry, plays and adult prose combine to make his children's books classics. His directness and simplicity, so much a part of his poetry and novels, are the essence of his excellence as a writer of children's literature, which must—before anything else—be understandable. His eye for accurate detail, so necessary for the poet, and his ear for speech, equally necessary for the dramatist, give his children's books a resonance few other authors can equal. But it is primarily his love of storytelling and his background of folk legends and myths, the essence of his early life and the study of his later years, which give him the easy familiarity which is the prime requisite of the storyteller. Children can discern affectation faster than adults, and are harder to convince than their parents that it should be tolerated. The enormous popularity of Padraic Colum's works among children is due to his genuine humility and the spontaneous outpouring of a gifted writer doing what he likes to do and what he does best.

Any overall survey of the life and works of a man who has lived so fully and so long, and has been so prolific, as Padraic Colum must inevitably only scratch the surface. The substantial individual contributions he has made to practically every area of literature tend to vanish into the sheer abundance of his productivity. This study has attempted to catalogue and evaluate Colum's works within the framework of their individual literary types. His poetry and drama have been treated perfunctorily by the critics, while his essays, novels and biographies have received scant mention. Of course, Colum is first a gifted poet, whose wide, continuing popular acclaim has not been matched with corresponding critical attention. The reason for this is that the apparent simplicity of the poems seems to leave little for the critics to say. But beauty in art comes from craftsmanship not accident, and this study has investigated Colum's poetry to see what constitutes this craftsmanship. Further it has attempted to survey the poems for trends and individual characteristics of content.

Colum's drama, while not nearly so important artistically as his poetry, had enormous historical consequence, and this is the path I have pursued most assiduously in the drama section. While none of Colum's plays were masterpieces, his uncanny ear for dialogue and the nuances of dialect were also to constitute enormous contributions to his narrative poetry and his novels, as well as his children's literature.

His essays, biographies and serious fiction, not unimportant in their own right as literary entities, provide us with our most complete picture of Ireland before and during a time which has proved to be of the greatest consequence in her history. His books capture the essence of the country peasant as Joyce's have of the Dubliner. Their methods were far different as is their ultimate place in literature, but judged in terms of their respective representations of Ireland, Colum's is the more comprehensive both in time and in substance.

His knowledge of folklore, begun at the workhouse and continued at his grandmother's fireplace in Cavan and on the road with his uncle Micky Burns, and later in the National Library and other libraries from New York to Paris to Honolulu, combined with his simplicity of style to form a natural artistry for presenting the mythology of the world, and especially Ireland, as a vital living thing rather than as a series of scholarly artifacts. His eminence as a translator of mythology for children is rivaled only by his other children's works and his poetry.

Buried deep in all of Colum's works is the author's own vision of himself, as storyteller and poet passing on the heritage of his own ancestry, country and world in a form as close as possible to the verbal tradition in which he was raised. His life reflects the image he has created for himself as an itinerant of the roads, now the roads of the world, telling his stories and poems again and again to students and children from Australia to Darien, Connecticut, stories of a land and an age in which he participated fully, along with their great-great-grandfathers, and stories of lands and ages remote and exotic to children of every age.

Colum's is the special magic of simplicity, truth,

humor, and, I may add, at the risk of seeming maudlin, *goodness*, that communicates itself clearly to children, who have always understood and appreciated him, and to those adults still among us for whom April is not "the cruelest month."

Notes

1 The Collumbs of Collumbkille

1. Unless otherwise noted, all quotations in this chapter attributed to Mr. Colum will be from a series of interviews taped during the period July, 1965 through March, 1968.
2. Mary Colum, *Life and the Dream* (Garden City, 1947), p. 95.
3. Padraic Colum, "Thomas MacDonagh and His Poetry," *The Dublin Magazine*, V, i (Spring, 1966), 41–42.
4. Mary Colum, pp. 174–75.
5. *Ibid.*, p. 6.
6. *Ibid.*, pp. 406–07.

2 Poetry

1. L. A. G. Strong, *Personal Remarks* (New York, 1953), p. 81.
2. *The Collected Poems of Padraic Colum* (New York, 1953), p. 127. Hereinafter page references to this book will follow the quotations and be designated CP.
3. *The Poet's Circuits* (London, 1960), p. 142. Hereinafter page references to this book will follow the quotations and be designated PC.
4. Strong, p. 79.
5. For a discussion of the Gaelic influences on Colum's versification techniques see Richard Loftus, *Nationalism in Modern Anglo-Irish Poetry* (Madison, Wis., 1964), pp. 178–81.
6. Conversation, April 3, 1967.
7. Padraic Colum, *Wild Earth* (Dublin, 1950), p. 35. Hereinafter page references to this book will follow the quotations and be designated WE.

8. Padraic Colum, *The Vegetable Kingdom* (Blooming-ton, Ind., 1954), p. 27.

9. I remember his giving a lengthy disquisition on the subject one evening as we sat in the Metropol Restaurant in Dublin drinking cocoa in a room literally filled with the world's most wholesome looking girls.

10. My colleague, Glenn Burne, has pointed out that the use of starlings here is reminiscent of Yeats's "The Wandering of Oisin," where starlings are used to recall Oisin to the world of mortal men.

11. He has told me that as a young Irishman he wrote an appropriate number of properly patriotic poems, but that now, mercifully, most of those have been lost.

Also, see Loftus, pp. 165–98. Loftus' thesis is that the underlying reason for Colum's poetry is to champion and glorify the peasant and his cause in Ireland.

12. Herbert Howarth, *The Irish Writers* (New York, 1958). This is one of the major premises of Howarth's book.

13. For an interesting treatment of Catholicism in Colum's poetry see Calvert Alexander, *Catholic Literary Revival* (Milwaukee, 1935), pp. 268–73.

14. Loftus, p. 191.

3 Drama

1. Una Ellis-Fermor, *The Irish Dramatic Movement* (London, 1939), pp. 188–89.

2. Cf., Lennox Robinson, *Ireland's Abbey Theatre* (London, 1951), pp. 49–50.

3. Cornelius Weygandt, *Irish Plays and Playwrights* (Boston, 1913), pp. 207–8.

4. L. A. G. Strong, *Personal Remarks* (New York, 1953), p. 82.

5. Andrew E. Malone, *The Irish Drama* (London, 1929), p. 39.

6. Robinson, pp. 25–26.

7. As quoted in Ellis-Fermor, p. 37.

8. *Ibid.*, p. 12.

9. Weygandt, p. 207.

10. Herbert Gorman, "Padraic Colum," *The New Republic,* July 21, 1917, p. 339.

11. As quoted in Padraic Colum, "The Talk of the Town," *The New Yorker,* June 9, 1962, p. 25.

12. Malone, p. 169.

13. As quoted in Lady Gregory, *Our Irish Theatre* (New York, 1965), p. 101.

14. Ellis-Fermor, p. 13.

15. As quoted in Weygandt, pp. 199–200.

16. Padraic Colum, "Ibsen and National Drama," *Sinn Fein*, June 2, 1906, p. 2, c.3–4.

17. As quoted in Robinson, p. 38.

18. As quoted in Stephen Gwynn, *Irish Literature and Drama* (New York, 1936), p. 176.
My remarks on the reception of the play are an abridgment of Gwynn's report.

19. W. G. Fay and Catherine Carswell, *The Fays of the Abbey Theatre* (New York, 1935), pp. 145–46.

20. *Ibid.*, pp. 146–47.

21. Padraic Colum, *Three Plays* (Dublin, 1963), pp. 6–7.

22. *Ibid.*, p. 35.

23. Weygandt, p. 204.

24. Ellis-Fermor, p. 190.

25. The play was originally called *The Workhouse Master*, but Lady Gregory asked Colum to change the title because she had written a play with the title, *The Workhouse Ward*, and she wanted to avoid confusion.

26. Colum, *Three Plays*, p. 176.

27. Conversation, October 20, 1967.

28. Colum, *Three Plays*, p. 142.

29. Padraic Colum, *Balloon. A Comedy in Four Acts* (New York, 1929), p. 46.

30. *Ibid.*, p. 107.

31. Especially interesting is a comparison of Caspar's final definition of the hero and Stephen Dedalus' final definition of beauty:

A hero is one who, when an event takes place, knows it for what it is—that it is that event and no other event . . . and, in order to be one with it, separates himself from all other things. In that act of separation the hero is made. And though nothing else has happened, that has hap-	In order to see that basket, said Stephen, your mind first of all separates the basket from the rest of the visible universe which is not the basket . . . When you have apprehended that basket as one thing and have then analysed it according to its form and apprehended it as a thing

pened. One is what one has done, and one is nothing else. (*Balloon*, p. 111)

you make the only synthesis which is logically and esthetically permissible. You see that it is that thing which it is and no other thing. (*A Portrait of the Artist as a Young Man* (New York, 1965), pp. 212–13.)

32. *Cloughoughter* manuscript, Library of State University of New York at Binghamton.

33. *Moytura*: *A Play for Dancers* (Dublin, 1963), author's note in front matter.

34. *Glendalough* manuscript, Library of State University of New York at Binghamton.

4   Fiction, Biographies, Essays

1. Padraic Colum, *Three Men* (London, 1930), p. 33.

2. Padraic Colum, *Castle Conquer* (London, 1923), p. 293.

3. *Ibid.*, p. 93.

4. Padraic Colum, *The Flying Swans* (New York, 1957), p. 1.

5. *Ibid.*, book jacket blurb.

6. June 16, 1957, VII, 5.

7. Colum, *The Flying Swans*, p. 114.

8. *Ibid.*, p. 10.

9. *Ibid.*, p. 1.

10. *Ibid.*, pp. 132–33.

11. *Ibid.*, p. 210.

12. *Ibid.*, p. 49.

13. *Ibid.*, p. 473.

14. *Ibid.*, p. 97.

15. *Ibid.*, p. 97.

16. *Ibid.*, p. 98.

17. *Ibid.*, p. 537.

18. *Ibid.*, p. 133.

19. *Ibid.*, p. 133.

20. *Ibid.*, p. 229.

21. *Ibid.*, p. 191.

22. *Ibid.*, p. 291.

23. It is interesting to note here that the name Ulick is an Irish form of *Ulysses*.

24. Colum, *The Flying Swans*, p. 154.

25. The cyclical passion-propriety dilemma of the generations is acted out in another family also. Mrs. Comyn's questionable relationship with Mr. Delaney causes her daughter to enter a convent and her son to run off to join the army.

26. Padraic Colum, *Ourselves Alone: The Story of Arthur Griffith and the Origin of the Irish Free State* (New York, 1959), pp. 11–12.

27. *Ibid.*, p. 127.

28. *Ibid.*, pp. 121–22.

29. Padraic and Mary Colum, *Our Friend James Joyce* (Garden City, 1958), pp. 118–19.

30. *Ibid.*, p. 79.

31. *Ibid.*, pp. 171–72.

32. *Ibid.*, p. 40.

33. Padraic Colum, *My Irish Year* (London, 1912).

34. Mills and Boon's catalogue at the end of Colum's *My Irish Year*, p. 2.

35. Padraic Colum, *A Half-Day's Ride: or Estates in Corsica* (New York, 1932), p. 7.

36. Colum, *My Irish Year*, p. vii.

37. *Ibid.*, p. 228, and Padraic Colum, *Cross Roads in Ireland* (New York, 1930), p. 287.

38. Padraic Colum, *The Road Round Ireland* (New York, 1937), p. 327.

39. It is interesting to note in this respect that his great concern with the evils of the exodus to America in *My Irish Year* and his preoccupation with it in his early plays were only the preamble to his own emigration from Ireland in 1914.

5   Children's Literature

1. Padraic Colum, *Story Telling, New and Old* (New York, 1961), pp. 13–14.

2. Conversation, February 15, 1968.

3. Colum, *Story Telling, New and Old*, p. 14.

4. *Ibid.*, pp. 4–6.

5. Front matter listings in later editions of Colum's works.

6. Conversation, February 15, 1968.

7. Lionel Trilling, "Mr. Colum's Greeks," *The Griffin* (Christmas, 1956), p. 13.

8. Conversation, January 1, 1968.

9. Padraic Colum, *The Children's Homer* (New York, 1962), p. 27.

10. *Ibid.*, p. 37.

11. Padraic Colum, *The Island of the Mighty. Being the Hero Stories of Celtic Britain Retold from the Mabinogion* (New York, 1924), p. 180.

12. *Ibid.*, p. xxi.

13. Padraic Colum, *Orpheus: Myths of the World* (New York, 1930), p. viii.

14. Padraic Colum, *At the Gateways of the Day* (New Haven, 1924), p. xvii.

15. *Ibid.*, p. xxvii.

16. *Padraic Colum, Legends of Hawaii* (New Haven, 1937), p. xii.

17. Colum, *At the Gateways*, p. 165.

18. Padraic Colum, *The Bright Islands* (New Haven, 1925), p. 225.

19. Padraic Colum, *The Big Tree of Bunlahy. Stories of My Own Countryside* (New York, 1933), p. 1.

20. Padraic Colum, *The King of Ireland's Son* (New York, 1962), p. 115.

21. *Ibid.*, p. 174.

22. *Ibid.*, p. 63.

23. Since this was written, *The Six Who Were Left in a Shoe* has been published (1968) by McGraw-Hill.

24. The catalogues published each year by the H. G. Wilson Company are the primary bibliographical tools for librarians' evaluations and choices of in-print children's material.

25. Padraic Colum, *The Boy Who Knew What the Birds Said* (New York, 1918), pp. 13–14.

26. Padraic Colum, *A Boy in Eirinn* (New York, 1913), p. xiii.

27. Padraic Colum, *The White Sparrow* (New York, 1933), p. 7.

28. *Ibid.*, dedication page.

29. Padraic Colum, *Where the Winds Never Blew and the Cocks Never Crew* (New York, 1940), p. 94.

The following list encompasses only those books written by Padraic Colum and does not include books he has edited or those for which he has written introductions and prefaces. For a more detailed bibliographical account of Colum's books as well as a listing of books he had edited and books to which he has contributed, see Alan Denson "Padraic Colum: An Appreciation with a Check-list of His Publications," *The Dublin Magazine*, VI, i (Spring, 1967), 50–67. Denson also includes a list of periodicals in which Colum has published. I would like to acknowledge the aid of the Denson bibliography in the preparation of the check-list which follows:

The Adventures of Odysseus, or *The Children's Homer*. New York, 1918, 1946, 1962; London, 1920.

At the Gateways of the Day. New Haven, 1924; London, 1924.

Balloon. A Comedy in Four Acts. New York, 1929.

The Big Tree of Bunlahy. Stories of My Own Countryside. New York, 1933; London, 1934.

The Boy Apprenticed to an Enchanter. New York, 1920, 1966.

A Boy In Eirinn. New York, 1913; *Sixth Edition Revised*, New York, 1929; London, 1915; Irish trans., Dublin, 1934.

The Boy Who Knew What the Birds Said. New York, 1918.

The Bright Islands. New Haven, 1925; London, 1925.

Castle Conquer. New York and London, 1923. An Irish translation was published in Dublin in 1939.

The Children of Odin. New York, 1920, 1948, 1962; London, 1922, 1929. An Irish translation was published in Dublin in 1936.

The Children Who Followed the Piper. New York, 1922.

The Collected Poems of Padraic Colum. New York, 1953.

Creatures. New York, 1927; London, 1928.

Cross Roads in Ireland. New York and London, 1930.

The Desert. Dublin, 1912.

Dramatic Legends, and Other Poems. New York and London, 1922.

The Fiddler's House. Dublin, 1907, 1909.

Flower Pieces: New Poems. Dublin, 1938.

The Flying Swans. New York, 1957. A German trans., *Ziehende Schwäne*, was published in Hamburg in 1960.

The Forge in the Forest. New York, 1925.

The Fountain of Youth. Stories to be Told. New York, 1927; Dublin, 1939.

The Frenzied Prince, Being Heroic Stories of Ancient Ireland. Philadelphia, 1943.

Garland Sunday. (A single broadsheet poem) Dublin, 1958.

The Girl Who Sat By the Ashes. New York, 1919, 1968.

The Golden Fleece and the Heroes Who Lived Before Achilles. New York, 1921, 1957, 1962.

A Half-Day's Ride: or Estates in Corsica. New York and London, 1932.

Heather Ale. 1907. No city, publisher information.

Irish Elegies. Dublin, 1958.

Irish Elegies. Second edition with substantial additions. Dublin, 1961.

Irish Elegies. Third edition with additions, Dublin, 1966; Chester Springs, Pa., 1966; London, 1966.

The Island of the Mighty. Being the Hero Stories of Celtic Britain Retold from the Mabinogion. New York, 1924.

The Jackdaw. Dublin, 1939, 1942.

The King of Ireland's Son. New York, 1916, 1921, 1962; London, 1920. Irish and German translations were also published, n.d.

The Land. Dublin, 1905. Also issued in New York, 1905.

Legends of Hawaii. New Haven, 1937, 1960; London, 1937, 1960.

The Legend of Saint Columba. New York, 1935; London, 1936.

Mogu the Wanderer; or The Desert. Boston, 1917; New York, 1923.

Moytura: A Play for Dancers. Dublin, 1963.

My Irish Year. London, 1912; New York, 1912.

Old Pastures. New York, 1930.

Orpheus: Myths of the World. New York and London, 1930. New edition, entitled *Myths of the World*. New York, 1959.

Our Friend James Joyce. (By Padraic and Mary Colum) Garden City, 1958; New York, 1958; London, 1959.

Ourselves Alone: The Story of Arthur Griffith and the Origin of The Irish Free State. New York, 1959. A Dublin edition entitled *Arthur Griffith (1872–1922)*. Dublin, 1959.

The Peep-Show Man. New York, 1924.

Poems. New York and London, 1932.

The Poet's Circuits. Collected Poems of Ireland. London, 1960.

The Road Round Ireland. New York, 1926, 1930, 1937. London, 1927. Macmillan.

Six Who Were Left in a Shoe. London, 1924 (in boxes, unbound); New York, 1968.

The Stone of Victory and Other Tales of Padraic Colum. New York, 1966.

The Story of Lowry Maen. New York and London, 1937.

Story Telling, New and Old. New York, 1961.

Studies. Dublin, 1907.

Ten Poems. Dublin, 1957.

Thomas Muskerry. Dublin, 1910.

Three Men. London, 1930.

Three Plays. Dublin and London, 1917. New edition, Dublin, 1963.

The Vegetable Kingdom. Bloomington, Indiana, 1954.

The Voyagers. Being Legends and Romances of Atlantic Discovery. New York, 1925.

Where the Winds Never Blew and the Cocks Never Crew. New York, 1940.

The White Sparrow. New York, 1933.

Wild Earth and Other Poems. Dublin, 1907, 1916; New York, 1916, 1922, 1927; London, 1923; Dublin, 1950.

Index